UNDERSTANDING FUTUROLOGY

UNDERSTANDING FUTUROLOGY

An Introduction to Futures Study

ALAN E. THOMPSON

David & Charles
Newton Abbot   London   North Pomfret (Vt)

303.4
T468u
1979

British Library Cataloguing in Publication Data
Thompson, Alan E.
  Understanding futurology.
  1. Forecasting
  301.2'4   CB158

  ISBN 0–7153–7761–2

Set by Trade Linotype Limited Birmingham
and printed in Great Britain
by Redwood Burn Limited Trowbridge and Esher
for David & Charles (Publishers) Limited
Brunel House Newton Abbot Devon

Published in the United States of America
by David & Charles Inc
North Pomfret Vermont 05053 USA

Contents

1 An Introduction to Futures

In the past few years there has been a great increase in interest in the future. The main reasons for this are a realisation that many of our present problems are a result of bad decisions taken in the past, coupled with the faster rate of change which is now occurring due to the cumulative effects of advances in science and technology. Also, there is a growing awareness that the future is not necessarily immutable, but to some extent we can choose the kind of future we have, and make value judgements on what we consider most desirable.

This book is intended as an introduction to Futurology, or Futures Studies, and is in many ways superficial. It is hoped that those who are already well into the field will be tolerant of the generalisations, the avenues left unexplored and the omission of detailed analyses. At this stage it is better to paint in the outlines with broad brushstrokes, leaving the individual to follow up particular areas according to his inclination. The bibliography, it is hoped, will be useful to those wishing to acquaint themselves more fully with the field.

For the same reason, numerical data have been excluded except where they are essential to the text, as also 'gee whiz' information. Most people are not very interested in figures, and they are not so easily amazed at the triumphs or otherwise of science as they were a decade ago.

It is to be hoped that this book will act as a starting point and serve to generate enough interest (or maybe sheer frustration!) to encourage readers to find their own fields of special interest. It is only when there is a large enough body of informed opinion, actively seeking change, that we will start to steer away from our present helter-skelter course—towards, perhaps, more desirable goals.

Perhaps it should be mentioned in this introduction that sometimes futures knowledge can come as something of a shock, and can have a disturbing effect for a while until the individual either begins to take positive action or adjusts so as to be able to ignore the information. If your world is defensively organised, and you do not adjust well to information that tends to disturb the *status quo*, then perhaps this is not the book for you. However, for most people the future presents a new challenge and, apart from some initial disorientation, most people seem to be able to cope with it. As more people become aware of the problems, and more positive action begins to be taken, the initial 'future shock'—to borrow a phrase from Toffler—will begin to lose some of its impact.

In conclusion, it should be said that the future is exciting, there are many good things that may be brought about by intelligently directed effort, and there are great improvements that may be made in the quality of our lives. Given the will, and the refusal to ignore issues in the face of difficulties, it is possible that we may push forward into a new age. Perhaps we will have to shed some of the things and ideas that we now consider essential, but in the process we may, in a sense, become more human.

At all events we must try, for if we do not it is unlikely that we will again reach the present high-water mark of our civilisation. There is no possibility of 'freezing' at our present level, for it is dynamically unstable; we must go either forward or back, and if we do go back it is difficult to see at what point we would level out, for we have come a long way in the past few thousand years.

Thus, like it or not, we are all in some sense committed to the future. Given this state of affairs it is perhaps reasonable that we should try to find out as much as possible about that future, or the choices of futures, as we can.

2 What is Futures Study?

To many people, futures study is something that is done with a crystal ball. As in other fields, more modern methods have taken over in the past few decades, although there is an element of crystal-ball gazing in some of the futures writing of the present time.

In this book, however, we are concerned with more mundane ways of arriving at some reasonable prediction of a future state. This is not to say that all prophecy is bunkum; there is good evidence that some prophets, biblical and otherwise, had a pretty good idea of what they were talking about. However, they did not leave an account of their methods, probably because they did not understand them themselves. At the present time there is no experimentally reproducible technique for seeing direct into the future and therefore science has nothing to say on the matter. Perhaps one day some of the fringe sciences dealing with this and allied topics will become respectable. If they do, this will be as a result of the protagonists evolving a repeatable and testable set of techniques and methods. The way is clear; all that are needed are the experimental results and maybe a little time to allow the rest of the fraternity to adjust to the new situation. There is no other way to build a body of scientific knowledge for, if a hypothesis is not testable, it is not science, however interesting it may otherwise appear to be.

What then of the methods that are used in studying the future? The principal one is extrapolation. Simply this means the extension in time of an observed trend. Thus, if we observe that the population of the world is increasing at a given rate, we can extrapolate and say that it will probably double in a given time. At the present time the doubling rate for population is once every thirty-five years. Or we can take the doubling rate for the use of power, which is once every fifteen years and probably slowing down.

Now doubling, or exponential growth, is something that cannot occur for long. Obviously there will come a time when there is no further room or scope for growth. Thus we can impose a limit to a trend. Population can expand only to the extent that there is food available for people to live, oil consumption can expand only to the extent that there is oil to be consumed, and so on. Perhaps the two most important things that a futurist looks for are trends and limits, for these set the overall framework for what is likely to happen.

From a knowledge of these it is possible to get a rough idea of an optimum; that is, either a best number or a best rate of use. For example, it has been suggested that the optimum number of people for the UK is around thirty millions; this is based on the number of people the land area can support. For the present, however, the British can still hope to import food in exchange for manufactured goods, and, indeed, within the framework of the EEC there is perhaps no good case for having each member country self-sufficient. In the long term, however, unless we can persuade other countries to halt their population growth before it is large enough to consume all the food they grow, this is the kind of number we are likely to be left with, assuming no new inputs by way of increased agricultural production or synthetic food.

This is not to say that we could not support a larger population: by banning most animal husbandry and bringing marginal and submarginal land into cultivation we could probably provide for another ten or twenty millions. However, the process would be sub-optimal in that some of the land farmed would be uneconomic, more time and energy going into the production of poor crops than would be available if those farming such land depended on their own crops alone without some kind of subsidy from the rest of the farming in the country. One could also arrive at a sub-optimal situation by having too few people, so that services operated inefficiently because they were under-strength or were

10

extended over too great an area. The formulation of optima is difficult as one has to arrive at them in part from value judgements. For example, how much space does a person need? A dozen people would probably give a dozen different answers, all more or less conditioned by their previous experience and temperament, although probably all would agree that people do need some space for recreation, set apart from the needs of agriculture, industry and housing. In general, while it is possible to specify within fairly narrow limits the physical requirements of people by way of how much food, what standards of public health, etc, they require, it is not so easy to specify the requirements that contribute to what we term the 'quality of life'. Significantly, these less definable requirements are the first to go in times of pressure, and they are generally the most sought-after once a person has achieved some measure of success and financial independence.

As well as optima for size there are also optima for rate of use. At first glance it might seem desirable to go for maximum use of raw materials, such as oil or metals, so as to give the fastest growth rate for the economy. Alternatively, it could be argued that they should be carefully husbanded over the longest possible time for, once used, there will be no more. Neither of these postulates is necessarily correct, yet presumably there must be some kind of optimum that will give the best results over the longest time. The argument for spreading resources over as long a time-base as possible is perhaps suspect, for it does not really matter if we use something quickly or slowly if all we do is to use it up for no end gain. The same argument can also be applied to population. Although it might in some respects be comforting if we could reduce the global population to a much smaller figure, there is really little to choose between having four thousand million people for the next hundred years or having four million for the next hundred thousand. Perhaps the first is more desirable for at least they will all be around at the same time and be able to communicate with one another.

What is important is what is done with a resource that will persist, or that will have its effect on the community after it is used up. Thus oil can be regarded only as a stepping stone to other things, and its use must be geared to other things that are happening in our society. Ideally, one could hope that its use will be so geared to progress in technology that it will begin to be superseded shortly before it runs out. If we use up oil and other fossil fuels too fast, then we are likely to be left with an unbridgeable gap in the technology. If we go too slowly, then the technology may never develop to the state where it is capable of making the progress necessary to bridge the gap. This kind of optimisation is difficult and, at the moment, no real attempts are being made to derive optima of this nature.

The study of trends and limits is a little mechanistic, almost as though we were caught up in some kind of machine where we could see what was going to happen to us next but had no power to do anything about it. Although much futures writing does have this kind of approach, it is not really what the game is all about. The primary supposition behind most of the work in futures is that we *do* have the ability to make some kind of change, although there is argument about its extent, and that we are not merely passengers.

This brings us to the idea of goals; that is, a proposed future state which can be aimed for. The putting of a man on the Moon was a goal, in this case a clearly defined one the achievement of which was largely a matter of technology. In some ways it was a simple proposition, inasmuch as most of the relevant information existed beforehand: all that was needed was the solution of a large number of technological problems, themselves easily definable, to see it through to achievement. This is not to belittle the efforts of those concerned, or the amount of time, money and care spent on the project. However, some goals are more difficult to achieve than this. The abolition of war is an example of a more complex goal. Here the problems are not wholly technical, the inputs are not so clearly defined, and there are emotive factors to be considered, as also the problem of what kind of power structures will be required in a society not geared to war, or at least to the possibility of it.

One further problem in futures studies is the unexpected and sometimes unexpectable input one may get from some new discovery in science. Although technology is in the main predictable, if only because it is geared to the solution of specific and defined problems, science is not. There is always the chance that some new discovery or invention will emerge and completely overturn predictions made by extrapolation or goal seeking. A new development in control of ageing would drastically alter population projections. A new power source would affect predictions regarding use of oil. The collapse of an animal or plant species could well have large-scale repercussions on food production, particularly if the failure came near the beginning of a food chain—for example, one of the few species of algae that are primarily responsible for food production in the sea.

There is little that can be done by way of making allowance for this in futures study, one can get some kind of idea of the rate at which unpredictable events occur, and it is a pretty safe bet that they will occur. But one cannot really guess what is likely to turn up in the next fifty years. All one can say is that *something* will, and that it will be quite strange measured by our present ways of thinking, with future consequences that are difficult to predict at the present time.

One possible lead to the anticipation of these new inputs can be got by examining the age old dreams of Man. Strangely, they often come true, although not in quite the way expected. Usually they are couched in magical terms, whereas their achievement is more prosaic. Thus, at one time, people thought that base metals could be turned to gold: nowadays we can in fact transmute elements, although the cost is so high that it is rarely worth doing unless there is a very large gain, such as in a breeder reactor for nuclear fuel. Again, men have always dreamed of flying: now we can fly, although the dream of a personal flying machine that can take off and land anywhere is attainable only for the few. Men have dreamed of being immortal, or at least of living for a very long time: now we know that ageing is a process that is perhaps retardable, and in the past few centuries we have doubled the expectation of life. Men have also dreamed of 'perpetual motion', or the creation of energy: presumably at one time energy was created, and if our science develops far enough to understand the process, it may well be possible to duplicate it. More recently, science-fiction writers have postulated the ability to traverse space without the necessity of passing through every single point from here to there and unconstrained by the limiting velocity of light: mathematically one can posit a multiply connected universe where such a thing becomes possible, and further research in gravity may identify a route, for there is some evidence that the speed of propagation of a gravitational field may be infinite—certainly it can escape from a 'black hole', from which nothing else can escape, and observably it can pass through a body the size of the Earth without the slightest diminution in strength as measured by the lack of effect of this 'gravitational shadow' on the Moon at times of lunar eclipse. Thus we can say that we have a force which does not interact with matter, it only acts on it; and, further, a force which does not interact with itself other than by simple addition. This can only be explained by recourse to another dimension over and above our three more usual ones, which brings us back to the possibility of a 'short cut'.

There are many other dreams that occur in the literature of all nations. Almost certainly some of them will be realised before the century is out.

3 The Need for Futures Study

The use of the plural when referring to studies of the future is deliberate. In considering the future we are really considering a series of choices or options, some more desirable or more probable than others. Thus, although there will actually be only one future, most futurists do not consider this immutable, but some kind of average result, compounded of all the interactions of all the choices and decisions of the present, set against the material constraints of the world in which they are made.

It is very necessary to know what options and choices are open to us, for things are not always what they seem, and what may at first glance appear to be a logical and desirable course of action may eventually lead into a double-bind situation from which we can neither retrace our steps nor proceed forward. Also, in the absence of some idea of alternatives, useful options may be missed, for any advance has momentum, and so often this momentum carries it past avenues that could profitably be explored.

Obviously people have always had some concept of the future, and made plans for it. Prehistoric man made provision for the winter, and planted against the expectation of harvest. One could made a case that any action is performed in the expectation of some future state. However, this is not quite the same as futures study. The significant difference is that whereas prehistoric man, and to a large extent his more civilised counterpart, thought in terms of one solution to one problem, the futurist thinks in terms of a whole complex of problems, and the effect the solution to one problem will have on the balance of the rest. In other words he is concerned with the dynamics of a system rather than a simple problem-solving activity.

Up to the time of the Industrial Revolution there was probably no great need to think in these more complex terms. By and large, Man was locked into a natural cycle of events that was not greatly disturbed by him. With the rise of technology, however, he began to influence this natural cycle of events in unforeseen ways, and to a much greater extent. Now we are in a position where we are effecting large changes in a short space of time and as yet we do not have any good method of predicting just where these changes will lead us. One can be pretty sure that they are not all beneficial, and some of them are perhaps fatal if we do not recognise them as such in time.

Thus we are faced with a situation where things happen more quickly, and with a greater effect than hitherto. However, our method of dealing with problems has not changed significantly to meet this. We still tend to consider problems in isolation, and apply remedies in isolation. We seldom even check back to see if the remedy did in fact have the intended effect, or whether it made things worse or triggered off some other problem in another field. In one sense, although we are often reminded that science and technology have given Man a greater control over his environment, we have less stability than before. At least, before the impact of technology, we could be reasonably sure that certain cycles in the environment would run themselves; now this is not so certain. The very last thing we want is total control, where we are responsible for every single change that takes place in the environment, for this would require a phenomenal amount of knowledge, constant monitoring and correction and a host of new values that we at present don't even dream about. We would be much better advised to interfere with the present natural cycles as little as possible until we are reasonably sure that we know what we are doing—before we release some new chemical or remove one more species from the face of the Earth. The biosphere is an intricately interwoven fabric, with its bases in the unchangeable past. If we lose a species there is no hope of recreating it, and every species

16

gone reduces the stability of the rest of the system, so that such continuing attrition can ultimately lead only to breakdown.

Futures study can act as a form of early warning system, whereby one can get at least some idea of the effects of an action before one has taken it. As the rate of change increases it is going to become more and more important to conduct good futures studies in more and more areas. For it still takes a person just as long to grow up, and perhaps slightly longer to become educated, as it did a hundred years ago. Now, however, there is no time for the next generation to supplant the old and gradually introduce new ideas. We must either retire people a lot earlier or train people to look further ahead and to examine in detail the probable consequences of their actions. Gone is the time when an education could last a lifetime. In some fields, a university degree can be obsolete within a few years, an event which may leave the holder at sea unless he is capable of adjusting to change and is to some extent forewarned of it.

Also, there is the cost-effectiveness of knowledge of the future to be considered. At the present time we are still putting up buildings that are capable of lasting two hundred years, only to spend money knocking them down again within twenty for some new development. Perhaps it might be better to consider a building in the light of its expected utility span, and design it so that either it will be nearing its demise at the end of that time or it can be demolished at low cost. Better still, it could be constructed so that it could be disassembled into its constituent parts and re-erected on some other site or in some other form. It would be possible to design a building now that could be assembled out of concrete blocks each weighing less than a tonne using a standard fork-lift truck. Perhaps the ultimate will be roofed cities using geodesic structures as designed by Professor Fuller. Having thus taken care of the climate (assuming they were not so big that their own climate did not start to operate inside the dome), the specification of buildings in the dome could be much less stringent to take care of the new set of conditions pertaining. At present, however, we still see building sites more reminiscent of preparation for the Aswan Dam or the Maginot Line, rather than a simple office block that may be obsolete or badly sited within a few decades. Generally speaking, the more mass one puts into something, the lower the level of the technology that is being used: aircraft are lighter than ships, and rockets lighter than aircraft; a Ming vase uses a good deal less material than a neolithic pot. Judged by this standard, building practice is still not far removed from the brute-force-and-ignorance stage.

The same can be said of road construction, with perhaps the exception of bridges. The Romans would have been proud of us could they witness our present efforts. Unfortunately, it is unlikely that the motor car will outlast this century, whereas some of the roads might well last another twenty centuries, or at least still show evidence of their intended function. For the amount of capital expended, and the amount of income lost by way of reduced crop yields, it might be better to design a new technology to get the transport of goods up into the air, or down pipes under the ground (virtually everything you buy in the supermarket could be made to fit down a ten-centimetre pipe). Quite often the thinking behind road construction is muddled. Usually they are built to 'ease congestion'—only to create more elsewhere. The fact is, of course, that roads do not cure traffic, they produce it. The average person is willing to spend some forty minutes getting to work, and whether he travels five kilometres or five hundred in that time is a matter of supreme indifference to him. Thus better road systems tend to result in people living further from their place of work and spending more money getting there. The result is a sterile urban sprawl, destructive of countryside and difficult to service.

In most areas of endeavour we are still following courses of action with little attempt to ascertain the secondary effects of such action, and quite often we do not later refer back to see if the primary goal has been achieved. This is obviously wasteful of time, energy and resources. It tends to produce quantitative rather than qualitative change and leads to an accumulation of secondary problems that are not easily soluble with good planning, and impossible without.

There is now becoming a need for a much more holistic approach, where a desirable state for the total system is postulated first and then adjustments made to that end, rather than an attempt at piecemeal problem-solving. It is this idea of a holistic model, coupled with systems dynamics, that will probably be of most value in the future.

4 Systems

A system may be defined as a set of interacting parts. Systems may combine to form larger systems, in which case they become subsystems of the whole. The term is used loosely in everyday language and most people have some idea of what it means. Ultimately, one could make a case that there is only one system, this being the Universe, and that all other systems are subsystems of this. We need not go quite as far, however. One should remember that we can *never* know the full relationships between all systems, because that very knowledge would greatly alter those relationships. This state of affairs is perhaps death to the fictitious 'detached observer' of pure science, but that argument need not concern us here.

Systems may be either open or closed. An open system has no end, while a closed one will come to an end in time, whereupon it may cease or repeat. If the Universe is infinite we could say that it is an open system—open, in fact, in both space and time. A closed system does have an end in both: one example of such a closed system is mining, for one starts extraction at one end of the seam or reef and finishes once one has come to the end of the commercially extractable material. Some closed systems are cyclic, however; for example, carbon dioxide in the atmosphere is removed by green plants, the carbon being used as an energy store and the oxygen being returned to the air. This energy is released again when the carbon is recombined with the oxygen, either by way of food for animals or by burning. Some of it may be sidetracked for a time into carbonates or coal, but on balance it cycles indefinitely.

Systems, however, can be more complex than this. Usually there is some kind of feedback in a system which controls its rate. For example, the deposition of the coal measures reduced the atmospheric carbon-dioxide content. This must have slowed plant growth and led to the development of plants with greater leaf area. Further, the availability of stored energy, represented by the differential between the carbon in plant material and the oxygen in the atmosphere, led to the development of animal life. Certainly there were no animals before this differential was produced, for there was no available energy gradient for them to run on (if one excludes those few bacteria who are capable of using inorganic substrates for their metabolism). Eventually these stores of energy triggered the Industrial Revolution, or at least powered it— and they still do to an extent of over 80%. Whether or not our efforts will eventually return us to a precarboniferous atmosphere and climate remains to be seen. If they do, then the probability is that the plants will cope with this new situation better than we will.

There are two kinds of feedback, positive and negative: a positive feedback accelerates the rate while a negative one inhibits it. Thus the extraction of coal in the early part of the Industrial Revolution led to more metal being smelted, more steam engines, more goods being produced and more people. This, of course, led to a vastly increased demand for coal, with some switch to oil later, although for our purposes we can consider it a similar substance. This process is still continuing, and it is axiomatic that any acceleration of processes in a closed system must bring the end of that system nearer in time. Unfortunately, much of our progress does just that. If somebody brought on the market a 'speed-up pill' that enabled people to dash about twice as fast and drop dead at thirty, it is doubtful if there would be many takers; indeed, it would probably be prohibited by law. However, an industrial process or consumer item that does just this to our dwindling resources is usually hailed as a boon to mankind. 'Progress', to be of any value, must have a defined direction and it is just this idea of progress being something more than a state of change that is lacking in our present systems.

The real problem, of course, is that our projected biological timespan, and in some cases even our personal lifespan, is

21

longer than the lifespan of some of the substances that we at present regard as essential to our civilisation. It is true, of course, that we can to some extent use substitutes—we can use plastic instead of tin for food preservation, aluminium instead of copper for wiring—but this is only begging the question for it will delay the crunch only until these substitutes too run out. (Also, they tend quite often to be less efficient, and their use in the absence of a solution to the primary problem will only mean worse trouble later.)

The theoretical answer is to get all materials in cyclic use, so that they are used and reused but never used up. This can be done by waste recycling, although at present the techniques are rather expensive and still lead to some waste. Some help may come from existing cycles here. A fair proportion of copper used is in the form of crop sprays that eventually end up in the sea. If copper could be extracted economically from seawater this would be a useful cycle to exploit, although it would not recover the solid metal that is buried in dumps all over the land. Increasing the price would help recovery, although it might also increase theft in the absence of other controls. Alternatively, one could avoid using copper in a situation where it was unlikely to be recovered. During World War II a major part of the American silver bullion reserves was used as wire in the windings of the Manhattan project separation plant. A surprisingly small amount was lost after the silver had been stripped down and recovered, which shows what can be done for an expensive metal under tight control. It is probable that a much smaller amount would have been recovered had the metal been used in a more disperse situation.

At the present time platinum, which costs more than a hundred times as much as silver, is used on razorblades and as a thin film on some kinds of switch contacts. The recovery is virtually nil because the amount used is so small. In systems dynamics terms we can say that there is no adequate feedback to prevent loss. Also we can observe that the 'marketplace' argument, which says that a reduction in supply results in an increased cost, which leads to economy and recycling, is not always effective. One result may be smaller and less recoverable amounts of material being used, with perhaps a greater overall wastage rate.

There is another avenue of escape by way of using lower and lower grade ores. By extrapolation, one will eventually come down to the average level of dilution of the sought-after material in the rocks of the Earth's crust. Here the problem will be solved, for no amount of throwing away can result in a lower level of dispersal than that; in fact, if one takes care to throw away anywhere but on the worked-out spoil heaps, it will increase the concentration of the desired material.

Unfortunately, the working of low-grade ore requires a correspondingly increased energy input, and this we are short of also. However, it does illustrate that shortages of material are to some extent illusory. One can never use a material up, except by a process of atomic fission or fusion, and even then one is only accelerating the natural rate by which it will be used up eventually anyway. When all the gold in the world has been mined, hoarded and lost again, there will still be just as much gold in the world as before, only its distribution will be different. Given the technology and the requisite energy, it could be recovered again, if it were thought to be worth it.

Thus the shortage of materials is really one aspect of an energy shortage and in thermodynamic terms accumulations of metals can be considered as accumulations of energy, for they represent a state of entropy, or randomness, less than the average state from which they were formed.

5 The Thermodynamic View

Everything is continually running down, people grow old and die, rocks weather and decay, even the stars must eventually burn out. The Greeks knew this and it appears in their philosophy, albeit in rather general terms. It was expressed more concisely by Maxwell, Carnot and others in the first part of the last century and gained its final form in the first part of this. There are three thermodynamic laws, which state that (a) energy can neither be created nor destroyed, (b) there is a continual running down of the system from high concentrations of energy to a more average distribution, this process being irreversible, and (c) entropy—that is, a state of disorder—decreases at very low temperatures.

The laws are empirical; that is, they are derived from observation and there is perhaps no good theoretical base for them. Observably they work, and so far nobody has been able to contravene them. Without going too much into the philosophical objections and bases to these laws we can assume that they are in operation through all levels of the natural world and our activities on it.

Originally the world probably condensed from relatively cold material which had never formed part of the main body of the Sun; this material was formed itself from the early, fast-burning stars of the Galaxy, which detonated and spewed their heavy elements across space. Since that time the world has warmed up, partly by the release of gravitational energy on compression and partly by the residual radioactivity of some of its elements. This has led to a molten core with convection currents exerting pressures on the crust. One result of this has been the uneven heating, folding and fissuring that has given rise to concentrations of metals.

Also, the Earth continuously receives a large amount of energy from the Sun. This causes the natural cycling of water from the atmosphere to the seas and back again, and also the planetary wind systems. Together, these agencies have been responsible for the less than random arrangement of different elements in the crust. Added to this there has been the effect of living things in concentrating material by way of carbonates, coal and oil deposits and oxygen.

Thus, although it is true to say that there is a trend to entropy in the sense that the total system is running down, the flow is not linear but turbulent. In rather the same way that some of the water in a fast-flowing and eddying stream will be going the 'wrong' way, some of the processes operating do not tend to entropy but result in accumulations of energy and less than randomly distributed materials. The power to effect this comes from the total system, so there is no overall gain, and the laws are conserved. The same kind of effect is observable in a refrigerator: it uses power and on balance it does more warming up than cooling down if one measures both the amount of heat removed from the cabinet and that rejected at the back. In the thermodynamic model of the world we can distinguish between the main flow and the eddies in a similar manner, and again we find that always the amount of energy used up in making some kind of differential is greater than that which can be released by running that differential down.

The interesting thing about this is that, whereas all natural cycles are powered by the main flow, or are at least so close to it that time out of flow is insignificant, most of our industrial processes are powered by releasing the power in the eddies. Thus food production is powered by the Sun *via* green plants, the food is eaten and the energy run to waste in, on average, less than a year. The fuel used to power industry has been out of circulation for several million years, however, and the same applies for most materials used by industry as well. This is the main problem facing our civilisation at the present time, for we are running down these accretions of energy and material at a far faster rate than they are accumulating. We have, in a sense, become parasitic on the mineral resources of the planet, and these have a far shorter expected lifetime than mankind's, or at least shorter than mankind's need be if we can find some other way of doing things.

There are three options open: we must get back much closer to the mainstream of energy flow from the Sun, which is, after all, very much greater than our present needs even if we consider only the minuscule fraction that falls on our planet; or we must try to duplicate the reactions of the Sun here, or at least get some kind of atomic reaction using a fuel that is neither scarce nor productive of dangerous wastes; or, finally, we must find some way of circumventing the laws of thermodynamics.

Surprisingly, all three may be possible. The total energy input from the Sun is vast and from our point of view inexhaustible. Given the technology we could use this until our civilisation died of old age, or until we ceased to exist in our present form. Direct solar radiation could be augmented by use of wind or wave power, as these are in effect concentrations of solar energy. Tidal energy could be used up to a point, although here we would be using gravitational energy, mainly from the Earth–Moon couple. At present the technology does not exist for these sources in any developed form, and when it does it is likely to cover large areas of ground (unless we get it up into space). However, the possibility is there and the main outlines of the technology are already known.

Thermonuclear energy from hydrogen fusion—duplicating the reactions of the Sun—is the present main hope. So far progress has been disappointingly slow. This is not because the reaction cannot be initiated; it already has, in hydrogen bombs. The problem is that it cannot be scaled down to a useful size. There is at present no known way of getting energy out of a small enough reacting mass to be contained in a power station. Laser technology may point the way here as this can give the intense heat needed to fuse atoms of deuterium or tritium. In a sense we have to do a good deal better than the Sun regarding the rate of energy release from a given mass. A roomful of Sun would give less heat than a

26

candle at a steady rate of output: the Sun is hot only because it is so big and every square kilometre of surface is the only outlet for over one hundred and fifty thousand cubic kilometres of reacting gas. Should it be possible to build a device which uses hydrogen from seawater as its fuel, then our energy problems are solved. The current alternative, that of fission power, using scarce metals such as uranium and thorium and producing long-lived and highly dangerous radioactive by-products, is scarcely a credible proposition for a long-term power supply. The total energy from these sources is less than that available from coal, to say nothing of the risks of waste disposal. However, we will probably be stuck with this for a few decades before fission power is phased out.

The third possibility, that of circumventing the laws of thermodynamics, is perhaps the most interesting. Firstly there is no such thing as an unbreakable scientific law. By their very nature scientific propositions cannot be proven in the absolute sense, they can only be disproved or not disproved, as the case may be. Usually they last for a while and are then overthrown or, more commonly, absorbed in a more embracing theory. The laws, furthermore, are empirical; that is, they describe what is observed to happen and say nothing of what might be made to happen with the use of a little native wit and imagination. Many of Man's artefacts are in fact new: for example, it is highly probable that a uranium fusion reaction moderated by graphite has never existed in the Universe before intelligence was applied to the problem.

If we examine our thermodynamic laws we will find that they are in fact self-contradictory. Either we must accept that energy (and that means matter, too) cannot be created or destroyed, or we can accept the fact that the Universe is in the process of running down from some state, which by reverse extrapolation must have been more 'wound up' than it is now. Ultimately our extrapolation must bring us to the creation of the Universe, which breaks the first law. If we postulate some cyclic Universe, which periodically runs down and then winds up again, we break the second law.

It is a pretty safe bet that matter was at one time created—
and could still be being created someplace in the Universe
today, for all we know. We can be fairly certain that it is
being destroyed in some fashion in black holes, or, if not
destroyed, then at least dropped through into another dimension rather as a stone may be dropped through the surface
of water. The true function of a black hole may, in fact, be
not much different from the hole in one's kitchen sink: all
we have to do now is to find the tap and we have in effect
an open system once more. Thus, the next stage after fusion
power might well be the *creation* of power. Similarly one
could hazard a guess and say that all processes are reversible
if only one knew how. There is some evidence that a gravitational field could be used to effect a selection between 'hot'
and 'cold' atoms of a gas, thus performing the function of
'Maxwell's Demons' postulated over a hundred years ago to
'wind up' a run-down thermodynamic system so that it could
provide an energy gradient once again.

It may be, of course, that these things are not possible,
or they may be a very long way in the future. However, it
is best not to prejudge the issue of possibility, for it is only
by believing all things to be possible that some things become
so. Also, with the present contraction of the timescale over
which science is operating, things which were science fiction
a few years ago are becoming old hat now. It would be a
great pity if science began to fossilise, and certain beliefs
were proscribed. We have had this situation before in religion
(and in science) and nobody benefited by it for any length of
time.

6 The Story So Far

The history of Man has been one of ever-accelerating progress. If we take one hundred thousand years ago as the starting point for *Homo sapiens*, we can trace the development of tools, agriculture and industry from this point. There is a definite trend towards sophistication of artefacts from the old to the new stone age, leading to the use of metals. This marks a turning point in technology, for metal implements were more durable than stone and they enabled Man to do more in less time than hitherto; also they were probably easier to make. This is a characteristic of technology: quite often the level of skill drops with a technological advance, allowing a greater sector of the population to benefit from it. This is not to say that there is any real regression; yesterday's skills become simpler to achieve, leaving time for the more complex skills of tomorrow.

Thus we find that reading is easier than listening and remembering, using a pocket calculator is easier than computation with pencil and paper, machine woodworking is easier than hand craftsmanship. This factor is often overlooked by those who wish to return to a more simple age. The level of skill in rural craft industries is often higher than in its modern counterpart and some people will never attain that level of skill. Technology is not about improved skill, but about finding quicker and easier ways of doing things. The rapid rise of the automobile was in part aided by the fact that not all people are completely at home with horses, and a car does not have a mind of its own or take a dislike to its owner.

This increase in the ability and speed with which things could be done had its feedback in population growth. Better hunting meant that more people could live in a given area, and predators could be wiped out. The demise of the sabre-toothed tiger was probably not unconnected with the rise of Man. Later, agriculture meant that even more people could

29

live per square kilometre and also led to settled communities as one had to be near one's crops to tend, plant and harvest.

The settled community led in turn to the greater specialisation of labour, so that new technologies developed more quickly. Pottery, weaving and metalworking diversified while ideas on civic structure, magic and religion probably developed and flourished in the close proximity of the early settlements. Writing was the next big step, as this put people more directly in touch with their past. This is important, for it is only with some idea of one's origins and traditions that a civic structure can be built. The next important step after the idea of keeping one's history is the planning of one's future. This development is really beginning to take place only at the present time. Doubtless in a thousand years it will be recognised as a turning point in the development of Man.

The Chaldean, Egyptian, Greek, Roman and finally our own civilisations followed more or less as a matter of course once the groundwork of settled communities with some form of government had developed. They rose and fell, but were in a sense the same civilisation; or, to take a different viewpoint, a striving to some half-seen goal, not clearly expressed, but real nevertheless. Without this goal-seeking on the part of some members of a civilisation it is doubtful if the structure would hold together for long, as there is always an opposite force at work. This tendency of people to think only of themselves, with no allegiance to any greater grouping, has triumphed in different times and places. Easter Island is perhaps a classic example, and the same sort of thing happened in the Eastern Mediterranean; the characteristics of this breakdown are that every family becomes an armed camp against the next. The tendency is always with us to some degree.

Up to the time of the Industrial Revolution the rate of change was relatively gradual: there was not much difference between the lives of father and son. Most changes were quantitative—things got bigger and better, with occasional reversals and disasters—but the pattern was fairly predictable. It is only with the coming of industrialisation that qualitative changes occurred fast enough to be noticed by all. The railway was perhaps the single great invention that everybody could see, and a great number of people used. Also, it was not difficult to guess what effect the railway could have on trade, particularly for a population that had previously found a trip just to the next village something of an undertaking. From then on the effects of technology snowballed, for technology is cumulative. The railways of course benefited greatly from the canals. Virtually all the technology regarding surveying, bridge-building, earth-moving—right down to the legal machinery for buying long thin strips of land—had been worked out by the canal companies; even the teams of labourers, thirty thousand strong, were in existence. And railways were easier to build than canals. They did not require waterproofing, headponds, locks or drainage, and they could even tackle moderate grades. Speeds and carrying capacity went up greatly, while costs came down. For the first time mass-produced cheap goods were available to a major sector of the population. With the coming of gas, electricity and the telephone we are beginning to enter an age that is recognisably our own.

It is easy to extrapolate from this point. We can talk of a future where machine power has taken over most of the work, where modern communications make it unnecessary to travel to the office, and where modern medicine has all but abolished disease and extended the lifespan to nearly a century. We can assume transport speeds will rise until no part of the world is more than an hour or so away, and that holidays will become a major preoccupation, with every family owning two houses and three cars.

Here, however, the dream has got ahead of the reality. So much futures writing has been pure fantasy, where the 'prophet' projects his desires without considering whether or not they are at all possible. Perhaps in the heydey of the Roman Empire one could have similarly projected that by some natural law of progress all people would eventually have an estate and a dozen slaves.

Unfortunately, the maths do not add up. If we take account of the natural limits of growth and permutation we see that it is just not possible. At the present time there is just not room for growth and we may shortly have to think in terms of recession. The Industrial Revolution was in part powered by the resources of the New World, by way of the fertility of virgin soils and the removal of forest from much of North America. This, combined with the iron and steel from England, meant that we were exploiting several hundred years of accumulated riches, and it will take as long or longer for them to accumulate again. Also, the Industrial Revolution is still exploiting natural resources, in the form of minerals, on a planetary scale. Here the period for accumulation is of the order of hundreds of millions of years, and there is no hope of ever accumulating this stock again.

There is only one avenue of growth left open to us, and that is a growth in efficiency. If we can make our present resources last ten times as long, then we have extended the timebase in which to find alternatives by that much. If we can get ten times the value out of a given amount of work, then we will be ten times richer. Essentially, any increase in efficiency comes from an increase in know-how, both at the scientific level and at the technical level of having men trained to make use of this new knowledge.

Surprisingly, a growth in efficiency should not be too difficult to achieve. The use of abundant resources has made us very wasteful; there is, in a sense, plenty of slack in the system that could be taken up. We can see this by looking at some of the things we have come to accept as everyday, without questioning their efficiency. A homely example is the electric light bulb. Of the power that goes into it, about 5% is manifested in the form of light; the remaining 95% is wasted in the form of heat. When heating is anyway required, this is not so important—other than that electricity is a wasteful way of heating; at other times it is pure waste and, even, additional electricity may be required for cooling if the heat has to be extracted after it is produced. Fluorescent lamps, on the other hand, can be 30% efficient, and it should be possible to achieve perhaps 50% without stretching the technology too much. Thus a tenfold increase might be possible if we really put our minds to it. Similarly, if we examine the system serving the electric lamp, we find a loss of 5% or over in the transmission system, and 60–70% conversion loss at the power station, which makes approximately twice as much waste heat as it does electricity. To this one must add the loss entailed in getting fuel to the power station, plus the capital cost in energy terms of the steel, concrete and copper used in the station and its grid system. We find that our home lighting is, at best, somewhat under 1% efficient.

Let us take another example, in case electricity is a special instance: the family automobile will do, as it is a common object on which a lot of design work has been lavished over the past few decades. To start with, of course, the engine is only 20–25% efficient, even if in peak tune. This is only part of the story, however: the average car weighs about ten times as much as its occupant, so only 10% of the energy used moves the occupant, the other 90% being used to move the car. Add to this the fact that under modern traffic conditions much of the energy is wasted in braking; compound it with the fact that road distances are quite a bit more than straight-line distances; make allowance for the fact that many journeys are made necessary by an unrealistic separation between work and living areas; and one comes out with a figure of about 0.5% efficiency for the automobile.

Home heating is another area we could examine. Here the efficiency is really zero, for all the heat put into homes leaks out again within a few hours. Thus home insulation can be a very effective investment in efficiency. Returns on capital can be as high as 30%, and capital appreciation will probably outstrip inflation. With the current investment rate of around 13%, against a depreciation rate of 20%—giving a net loss of 7% before tax losses—the investment is a very attractive one indeed.

Thus investment in increased efficiency is an obvious way of advancing a society that is running into growth problems.

One aspect of technology is that it has generated its own mystique. People *like* mystique—one of the attractions of magic is the 'unknown' aspect of it. Now that magic is believed in less than before people have sought in technology a source for their need to be awed. Quite often, people do not want to know why their technological possessions actually work. The new automobile owner will boast of its performance as though in some measure it rubs off on him. He will tell you that it can do 160kph, although the speed limit is well below this for most countries, and one's real average for all journeys a bit below 50kph. Add to this *the time taken to earn the money to run the automobile*, and the true speed comes out at around about 15kph, somewhat slower than a bicycle.

Airlines run into the same sort of difficulty if one examines their claimed speeds in this manner. If one flies from London to New York, one will do it in about five hours at a speed of about 1,000kph. Progress indeed! Unfortunately, one is likely to spend at least a couple of hours getting to the airport; then one has to wait an hour after check-in, and spend perhaps another couple of hours getting from the airport to one's destination on the other side. The average speed has already dropped to half that of the 'plane. Worse is to follow, however; if one takes the average working wage we find that it takes nearly a month to earn the money to make the flight, and this brings us down to something approaching the average speed of a sailing ship. One can quibble with this sort of comparison, of course, but in its own way it is just as valid as the picture given by the advertisers who wish you to spend your money. Although technology does, of course, bring benefits and advantages, these are quite often less than we have been led to believe, because there is considerable inefficiency built into the system.

It may be argued that, while it is all very well to examine the efficiency of a particular machine, the technology does not exist to improve it. The short answer is 'go and get some more technology'. But it is, of course, true: the normal car engine could not easily be made to be more efficient than 25% although diesel engines achieve 40%, and 50% is possible using steam generation from the exhaust to produce a return pressure for the pistons. The point is that technology has not developed towards economy because there has been no pressure for it to do so. A policy of almost free energy has led to its very wasteful use; with shortages now becoming apparent we are likely to see the 20kpl (60mpg) automobile within a couple of years, and a rationalisation of use could halve again the petrol consumption. Similarly, for other parts of the technological superstructure, there is a great deal of fat to be pared off before we run into fundamental limits, and even these can often be reduced by using resources in a slightly different way.

Thus it appears that we are at some kind of watershed in the history of our development. The period of growth is all but over; if we continue to aim in this direction we are courting disaster for, once we overrun the available resources, the crash will be sudden and will bring down not only the industrial infrastructure of our society but much else also. The real risk, of course, is not that we will get poorer, or yet that the expectation of life may go down instead of up, but that we may lose some of our hard won knowledge. If our civilisation collapses to the point where our institutions of research and learning can no longer operate, then the collapse will be cumulative. Further, it is unlikely that we will be able to rebuild this structure, for it was a capital asset bought by the use of resources that will not be available again. True, we might be able to take off in some other direction as yet unseen, but, if this new direction and new set of values are to evolve, it is more likely to do so from the springboard of our present position rather than from some lower level resulting from the wreckage of a collapsed civilisation. There are plenty of small groups and tribes about the world existing with a small store of knowledge and a low level of technology: they have been around for a long time and they have not made any advances of note; it is unlikely that we would do any better if we get ourselves into a similar situation.

The most obvious route at the present time is a swing from the extensive use of energy and materials to an intensive use. This is already happening—a modern transistor radio is about one-hundredth of the size of the kind of receiver that was used forty years ago, and uses far less metal. A modern computer can handle several thousand times the paperwork that a single girl with a typewriter did a few years back, yet it uses far less metal and building space than a thousand girls with typewriters would. This is, of course, nothing new in the development of Man: agriculture produced hundreds of times as much food per square kilometre than hunting did; factories increased the production of the individual very greatly; and transport systems have greatly increased the amount one person can move from place to place. Thus an investment in greater efficiency is only an extrapolation of a trend that has been with us for some time now.

7 Environmental Impact

Generally speaking, most natural systems are stable—at least if considered over the short term. Thus, if one particular species increases due to a chance or cyclic increase in food supply, then it will not be long before predators or, possibly, disease increases also and pushes the population back towards the mean. If a system did not have these checks and balances it would not persist for long: the chance of our being able to identify such an unstable system, in our short space of time, is remote. However, this is not to say that natural systems are stable in the long term: of all the species that have existed most are now extinct and, presumably, at some future date all of today's species will become so.

Onto this very slow procession of natural change we have imposed a much faster tempo. The rate of extinction of species at the present time is higher than it has ever been. This is worrying because we too are a species, and consequently every extinction of a species can be considered one step closer to our own extinction.

The reasons for this increase in the rate of change have their roots in the Industrial Revolution, although there was some impact before that time. The causes are twofold: the deliberate (and accidental) extermination of species to make way for increased farming land; and the disruption of the biosphere by chemical inputs that it cannot handle.

The loss of the wolf and the bear were, to the UK, a cause for relief—although it is perhaps a pity that there are not a few wild areas left where they can roam. Other countries seem to have come to terms with their larger animals, at least until the pressure for land asserts itself. The loss of species of butterflies and moths, with the great diminution in numbers of others, is a cause for regret, as also is the reduction of plant species that is now occurring. If we push the scale a bit further we may begin to remove more fundamental elements

37

of the food chain which culminates in us. Already there is evidence that soil fertility cannot be maintained indefinitely with current methods of high fertiliser input as this practice tends to decrease the soil bacteria and reduce the humus content, leaving the land more liable to erosion. The East Anglian fens are a particular example of this.

If we continue to dump waste in the sea at the present increasing rate, sooner or later something nasty is going to happen. While the pollution of the Great Lakes and the Baltic are a cause for concern, the pollution of a major ocean would be a cause for real panic. The food loss would be huge and the atmospheric consequences global in scope. However, this is the direction we are headed in and, failing some moderation or negative feedback in the system, this is where we are going to arrive sooner or later.

The main problem of chemical inputs is that the chemicals are usually of a kind not found in nature, and therefore there are no organisms capable of dealing with them. True, given time, bacteria would probably evolve to break down most plastics and other chemicals, but the timescale is too short for such an evolution to take place. In some instances, chemicals can be tailored to suit existing bacteria. Detergents are an example of this: the early ones were not biodegradable and led to foaming problems in rivers; later ones were made biodegradable and therefore do not persist long enough to give a foam problem. There is evidence that this may be just sweeping the problem out of sight, for many modern detergents encourage bacterial growth by the very fact that they are a foodstuff for them: this can lead to a great increase in bacterial numbers which may alter the biochemical balance of a waterway.

One of the most publicised chemicals is DDT. It is a persistent chemical which eventually ends up in the sea. Here its most obvious effect is that it gets absorbed by plankton, concentrated in the fish they feed, and concentrated yet again in birds that prey on the fish. This leads to a reduction in shell strength so that hatching becomes impossible. There are almost certainly other effects we do not know of—as yet, we have picked up only the more obvious ones. The maximum concentration of DDT in the sea resulting from use to date may not occur for another twenty years; even if production were halted now the story is by no means finished, despite the fact that production has been cut back in the past few years.

In addition to detergents and DDT there are many thousands of other new chemicals loose in the environment, all with potentially unknown effects. True most are probably harmless, but the statistics of risk are overwhelming if one extrapolates the trend indefinitely. Even the kind of testing given to drugs is not adequate, as is evidenced by the thalidomide disaster; yet most new chemicals are tested much less carefully than drugs are.

It is probably true to say that any new chemical will have *some* effect *somewhere* in the system, and it will take a very long time for the system to adjust to the new input. The first obvious adjustment is the reduction or extinction of a species, and this in turn will have a 'shunt' effect on the others. Disruption is caused not only in the organic world: freons, which are used in spray cans, are persistent in the atmosphere and can catalyse the breakdown of ozone in the upper atmosphere. As the ozone layer is our shield against ultraviolet radiation, this breakdown is obviously something to be avoided. Life did not get established on the land until this shield was extant; at worst, if it goes, the surface of the Earth could be sterilised by the incoming ultraviolet radiation. At the present time, production of freons is in the region of a million tonnes annually and increasing. No doubt it would be possible to reverse the trend by introducing some other chemical to breakdown freons, or catalyse the formation of ozone, but this is no way to run a system that is perfectly capable of running itself in the first place.

The roots of the problem lie in a conflict of interest in the industrial system. Even when the facts are known—and we don't know ten per cent of them yet—it is difficult to get a corresponding reaction to introduce negative feedback into the system.

The conflict of interest is between what a company is set up to do, and what is the most desirable thing for the populace at large. A company must operate profitably or it dies: this is the system by which our production operates and, in many ways, it is a good thing, for it removes unprofitable businesses which might otherwise waste a lot of material—and waste a lot of people's time for low wages and perhaps a negative amount of effective work. Even in communist countries the system is more or less the same: there is always an incentive for more efficient production in terms of goods got out for work put in. But no matter how concerned a company may be, and no matter how well its management is informed, it cannot take antipollution measures that will price it out of the market, for if it does so it will fail and its place will be taken by a competitor—perhaps from another country where the rules don't apply—who will continue to work in the same way and so produce the same problem as a by-product.

There is, therefore, a requirement to alter the dynamics of company operation so that it becomes economic to reduce or obviate pollution. The best method so far is 'polluter pays' legislation. This, to be really fair, should be backed by a total ban on imported goods from competitors who do not run by the same rulebook, with pressure to get the rules established on a global scale as soon as possible.

There would also be a case for refund on exports by companies operating the rules. This might mean that some countries would be subsidising the clean-up operation, but some kind of inequalities are bound to occur in the initial stages before there is general acceptance.

Basically 'polluter pays' legislation means that the consumer (not the Company, as is often thought) pays for the cost of the pollution, or the cost of avoiding it. This might lead to a cessation of trading on the part of some companies—if this happens it is a good thing. Many companies, of course, run at an overall loss to the financial system, although they themselves show a profit. A badly designed pulp mill leaking mercury waste into a river may run at a profit of so many hundred thousand per year, but in the process may destroy a fishery worth twice as much; thus the pulp mill apparently runs at a profit, but the overall effect to the system is a loss.

Atmospheric pollution in cities costs millions in crumbling stonework, lost working days, hospital beds and so on, with probably as much loss by way of reduced agricultural production outside. If this cost were borne by the factories producing the pollution they would probably prove uneconomic. Usually the cost of removing the pollution is less than the cost of the damage it does, so the system can be brought back into profitability again without too much industrial disruption. The net effect may be a (temporary) reduction in the real wages earned by the community coupled with an increase in the quality of life. In the long term, the removal of uneconomic industry will result in a rising of real wages. In cases where an industry must close, there will, of course, be some temporary disruption of the labour market, but this could be avoided by phasing; and, even if the worst did happen and people lost jobs, it is still better to pay them for doing nothing than to pay them for doing what is essentially negative work.

8 Time and Free Will

The free will *versus* determinism argument has been with us for a good many thousands of years. Basically it is not a soluble one inasmuch that, if our actions are predetermined, then we will either believe or not believe this according to our particular determinism; similarly, if we have free will we can believe it or not according to how we use that freedom. Of all the possible permutations it is probably best to believe that we are free, and that the choice is free. There is really no good proof one way or the other: all one can say is that, the greater the belief in freedom, the greater the progress of a civilisation at the time that the belief is strongest.

In actual fact, as in most things, there is probably a bit of both at work. We are obviously not free in some things—we are all going to die, for example—and we can behave only in accordance with natural restraints, although these can be pushed back as we acquire a greater degree of know-how. One could make a case that 'all things are possible to those that believe', given the will and sufficient time and effort. At the present time, however, we need to recognise our immediate areas of freedom and exploit these, for therein lies our greatest hope of progress. If we find that an end, no matter how desirable, is not achievable with our present state of knowledge and organisation, then we had better make plans for something else, setting it aside as a long-term goal to be kept in mind for later achievement.

One such long-term goal is with us in the apparent desirability of raising the standards of the Third World to that of the West: as a practical proposition we had better put it aside for a while, for the materials and energy are just not available—and, even if they were, the pollution burden incurred under the present way of doing things would be unacceptable. We will be hard put to maintain our own standards for very much longer without attempting to raise those of others. What is needed, of course, is some kind of system that will gradually share out the wealth so that we eventually come to some more equable distribution.

It is a truism that what the rich have in one generation the poor expect to have in the next . . . or at least shortly after. This is true of most things, from brick houses to automobiles. In the next generation the rich are likely to experience a rapid dissolution of capital and perhaps effective bankruptcy for many, so perhaps this is the realistic expectation of the poor also. In simple terms, we cannot do very much to raise the living standards of the Third World because we haven't really done so well in raising our own. True, we have made progress in the last century, but this was by exploiting new land and materials; these have now been exploited to the limit and there is no way of calling them back again. The only way we can be reasonably sure of improving the lot of the Third World is by developing technologies that will be suitable for the conditions pertaining there. To assume that we can effect an improvement by transferring our present technology is a form of arrogance: our present technology is barely adequate to meet our own problems and, quite often, by trying to graft it onto an alien root we end up making things worse, not better. The problems in developing countries are complex, and piecemeal efforts, by way of boreholes, medicine and free food, are just as unsuccessful there as they are here. The effects are usually worse because there is less slack in the system with which to cover inefficiency.

This is not to say that some good work is not being done. The need is now beginning to be seen in terms of trying to understand how things work initially and then adjusting the system inputs so as to get a real gain. We have already come a long way from the response of a few years back when one merely sent a gunboat full of corn and medicine. There is perhaps still some arrogance in our assumption that our form of civilisation is best—for, after all, our own way of doing things may in the long term be less viable than the system that we are attempting to replace. In many cases we might do best to let well alone until we really know what we are about. This, of course, might well lead to criticism. It has been said that the West will not help the Third World, and is in some way wicked for not doing so. The truth is much worse than this. In many areas we *cannot* help the Third World because, let alone the will, we lack the knowledge. However, our pride is such that we would sooner be painted as villains than fools, if we have to make the choice. Thus desirability and emotional involvement are not necessarily good criteria for action. We must learn to distinguish what we can do from what we want to do before embarking on a course of action, for we can operate only in areas where we have freedom, and these are usually the areas where we have most knowledge.

The concept of free will was eroded by the advance of science in the last century. By the middle of the nineteenth century it appeared that we were well on the way to a mechanistic theory of the Universe as some kind of clock. The problem was inherent in the atomism of the Greeks for, if all change is caused by the movement of the atoms, then once given its starting momentum it should logically tick over to its conclusion. Chance and randomness exploded this view, and things became more uncertain, although the rules of chance cannot really be said to apply in an infinite Universe, for a large number of chance events will give some statistical average. We could, however, make a case for mind being able to exploit chance, and take it off in some direction that deviated from the statistical average, in rather the same way that a Geiger tube takes a chance electron and multiplies it into a definite pulse.

Within its limits, the mechanistic view is probably correct. Given the right mix of elements, and the right temperature and timescale, it was probably inevitable that life would develop on Earth—or any other Earth, for that matter—and that at some later time it would become self-aware and reflective. If we concede this much then we might as well postulate that eventually life will, inevitably, develop free will,

44

although there is not really any good mechanism postulated for this as yet. Certainly, we can observe that some sort of process is in operation, one which tends to a greater degree of complexity of organisation that in Man has led to the development of the brain in a rather short time (biologically and palaeontologically speaking). As yet, we do not really know the beginnings of this process and cannot guess its ends. By extrapolation we can see that if it continues we may eventually become the heirs to space and perhaps spread throughout the Galaxy. We could develop our art and science to heights undreamed of, or we could go into extinction making the evolution of the brain a comparatively minor side track in the overall path of evolutionary development—some minor, self-correcting mistake if you like.

For the present, the picture looks hopeful if we can get over the hurdles of the next fifty years. As a species we are young indeed and should have a good few scores of millions of years ahead of us, perhaps then forming the nucleus from which the next dominant lifeform evolves. We ourselves are not some special one-off creation, although we sometimes behave as though we were. If we look at our various parts we realise that they evolved at separate times and diverse places: our nerves and eyes developed in the primitive seas; our skeleton took its present form as we crawled onto land; our sex hormones we share with the plants, they are so very old, while the loss of hair is probably quite recent.

One could postulate that our essential human-ness might well persist long after the species had changed into something else, that it would be handed down as something worthy of preservation, so to speak, along with the brain and nervous system. Einstein once said that he could think of no better end of a theory than that it should be preserved as some special case in a better one. Who knows, perhaps those things which we now value could after all be eternal, if only because they are a necessary and desirable attribute of life. (This, of course, is pure speculation and does not really form part of the mainstream of futures thinking; however, it is not a bad thing to speculate in a dozen different ways, as one of them is likely to be somewhere near the truth.)

One other interesting side-effect of the concept of free will is that it presupposes certain structures in time. Retrospectively, of course, there is no such thing as free will. One has made a certain decision and one must stick with the results: one cannot go back and try the other path or, if one can, one cannot take the knowledge of this one along for comparison —which amounts to the same thing. In the future, however, we do not posit one unalterable line, although certain things may be unalterable. Thus we are, in fact, making a model that is branching in time. To some extent the branches intersect, so that if one goes off course, one can work back to certain desired ends, although with a slightly different set of memories and a slight displacement in time compared to the direct route. Time, therefore, must be represented as something other than a straight road down which we are carried. At the very least we must consider it as a plane (or plain?) with a choice of roads over it. Inertia still applies, of course: in a short space of time it is possible to make only small changes, but by a cumulative pressure we can arrive at very distant places from our straight-line course. In a way we are rather in the position of a tanker captain: the bigger and faster tankers become, the further ahead he has to plan his actions. As our civilisation becomes bigger and faster, our old tug-boat handling skills become more and more outmoded.

We can further extend our model of time to make it three-dimensional; this gives us an infinite number of routes to a host of slightly different tomorrows. It should be realised that this is only a model, designed to give the idea of choice, alternative futures and progress. Within its limits, however, it is a useful concept. We can get the idea of inertia, the idea of an act of will bringing a person or a group to some position that would not have been attained by freewheeling. It can also give an idea of the impossible, inasmuch that any desired state that is either behind one or at such an acute angle that one cannot make the turn is impossible to achieve. Further, it shows the need for forward vision in the form of futures studies, for without this we are travelling blind in a fog and may not realise danger until it is too late; or, for that matter, see the promised land until we have passed it by. With increasing speed of change we must eventually arrive at the point where futures knowledge becomes essential.

9 A Code of Ethics

Much of futures studies consists of a series of trade-offs. The idea of a coming Utopia where everything will be perfect is fast disappearing; indeed, much futures writing has tended towards dystopia, where everything is about as bad as it can be. This latter concept is, however, probably equally unrealistic. What will probably happen, as people become more aware of the options open, is that some kind of average result will come about, where some things get worse and others better. Hopefully our civilisation will continue in some form and achieve higher values than at present, although this progress may not be even—and we may have to go through some kind of crash first.

What is needed is some yardstick to measure what is desirable and what is not. In any postulate for the future one must have starting premises, for without these there is little point in starting at all. Without being too exact one can state broadly that a course of action that will improve the lot of Man is desirable and one that will give the reverse is undesirable.

It is difficult to spell out in exact terms what are the real requirements of Man, but it is possible to get a good working agreement without going too much into the *minutiae*. One must add a rider to this, inasmuch that a course of action that will improve the chances of survival of the species is desirable, and one that will decrease those chances is not. Logically, the survival of the species should have priority, thus the second provision acts as a limiting clause on the first.

There are good reasons for arriving at these premises, for it is easy to get agreement that improved standards of housing, education, health and nutrition are desirable. Also, the desire for the survival of the species exists at an instinctive level, whether people openly admit to it or not. Thus these are good working premises as they can be applied by common consent.

48

Unfortunately, the two premises are often in conflict. It is precisely the desire that conditions should be improved that has led to the threat to the environment and resource-base that culminates in a threat to us. Therefore it is necessary to get some kind of trade-off of the present against the future. Thus there is a real need for some kind of ethic, or perhaps ethos, which can define acceptable routes to desired goals. Although there is apparent conflict today between resource use and standards of living, this is to some extent artificial in that what is really wrong is our technology. Given a better understanding of how to achieve our aims, we could still raise living standards without threatening the environment. The problem is in some ways similar to problems encountered in engineering, where things do not scale as we want them to. Thus one cannot double the height of a building without making the walls thicker and ending up with less than double the floor space. One cannot scale down a thermonuclear reaction and still get it to work. Similarly, we cannot extrapolate and say that every person on the globe should have an automobile, because the number of square kilometres of road and parking space required would seriously threaten agriculture, while the fuel base on which automobiles run would probably not last as long as the expected lifetime of an automobile in any case.

The new technology must be designed to be simple, effective, and not extensive in resource use. Partly the problem has been created by the poor wanting what the rich observably have, and in many cases attaining it in a relatively short time. This could be used as an argument for not having rich people, although it could equally be used as an argument for a different set of expectations for the poor. There is, perhaps, nothing wrong in a successful person who may have invented some new process or service that by its use has saved millions of working hours, or perhaps reduced suffering, having his own private aircraft, the better to attend his business. To extrapolate and say that within fifty years everybody should have a private aircraft is not realistic; even if achievable it is not desirable. The situation at present is that civilisation is observably advanced by the efforts of relatively few individuals, some of whom may end up with a greater-than-average share of wealth as a result of their efforts, while the bulk of the new wealth is shared out more or less evenly, thus improving everybody's lot. There is no corollary that says everybody must end up as rich as the richest in the community; they may or they may not, but even if they do this does not mean that they should, or in fact could, spend their wealth in exactly the same way. It should, of course, be added that there are other ways of getting rich that may in fact depress everyone else's standard of living, but this will be dealt with in the next chapter.

Straight extrapolation is not much use in planning for an increase in wealth and it can be a dangerous tool if the alternatives are not considered. Perhaps the best alternative would be to design a society where one reduces the outgoings of the average person, rather than increase the paper money going to him. By taking the average household budget, halving the need for expenditure on gas and electricity, reducing the running cost of a car and maybe reducing the working week to four days so that the householder can grow a little food, or reduce the amount of labour brought in, one could reduce the cost of living. This could all be done by application of not much more than the present technology and there is already some movement in this direction.

There is much to be done in the field of values and ethics. It is at present a neglected field, for there is not the large cash input from business institutions as there is in other fields. Also, it is a more open system in that there are fewer material constraints to channel thinking. The need is just as real, however, for our value judgements condition the actions we take in the material world. At present it may seem crazy to try to interest the average man in such presumptuous ideas as the lifetime of the species when all he is really concerned about is where the next meal is coming from. The quick answer is that, in the West at least, the average man need not worry too much about

50

the next meal . . . but if he does not get some reasonable idea of the future he may have to, pretty soon.

Another factor is that people do need some kind of security. It is better to live in a society that at least *thinks* it is going somewhere, even if the view is a little fuzzy round the edges. Most people would prefer to think that they were contributing in some way to an advance in society, and that our human values of justice, love and a greater understanding of the natural world were in the ascendant, even though one might be in a difficult patch at the present time. These are the kind of ideals that give people cohesion and enable them to work together. Once vision is lost one ends up with a free-for-all where everybody tries to grab what they can, only to discover that the division of the parts ends up as much less than the sum of the whole. Man is not merely pushed forward, like toothpaste out of a tube—there is at least an equal amount of pull from his visions and his dreams. It is this very fact that may give us our dimension of free will; all the time we are driven by the unalterable past we are operating in a deterministic way. If we are being pulled by a variety of possible futures then we have a more open system to play with. The point at which Man tips from being driven by what has happened to being pulled by what might be made to happen is perhaps a watershed in human development. The only way we may make the transition is by a greater knowledge of the future. It has been said that knowledge is power; better yet, it may be freedom.

10 Wealth and Growth

To most people wealth means money, but the two are not the same. We can speak of mineral wealth or wealth in industrial investment or expertise. Up to a point, the two are interchangeable, one with another, but only so far as the monetary system works and is not strained to a greater extent than it can adjust to. What, then, does money represent? For the man in the street it represents goods and services which he can buy. In some ways, it can be considered as a method of storing work: thus one can do work for others in exchange for money and, at some later time, exchange this money for work done by others for oneself; one can delay the benefits of working until such times as one wants them, as for holidays, retirement and so on.

Money in itself is not stored work, however, it is merely an artificially produced commodity, in restricted supply which, by common consent, is agreed as being representative of work.

Work is, of course, not the only way of getting money. Interest is another method of transfer. This probably has its roots in farming. If one farmer borrows from another a bag of corn at seed time, it is perhaps reasonable that he should give a little more than one bag back at harvest. Thus interest represents a part of the gain made by the use of money over a time. This, one must presuppose, means that a gain has been made: if the money is used in such a way that a loss is made, then ultimately, in terms of the whole system, negative interest occurs and the lender gets back something less than he put in. In practice this seldom occurs except in the case of company bankruptcy: more commonly the result is spread through the system and hidden by inflation. Thus it will be seen that, when the monetary system is expanding, there are profits, and when it is not there is inflation. Of course there may be both profit and inflation at the same time, and here we must look for the net effect.

There are several ways in which the system may grow, only two of which are desirable and perhaps only one practicable. Firstly, of course, the monetary system may get bigger by virtue of a greater number of people using it. Thus, if one doubles the population, one can print twice as much money, but if there is no corresponding increase in goods and services it will be worth only half as much. One can gain some cushioning effect by inflation, for, if one halves the value of the monetary unit, one has in effect called a lot of capital back into circulation, because those people and institutions who have saved money will have their future potential demand on the system halved—thus some capital is being used as income. This is a potentially dangerous state of affairs, for whereas it is perfectly reasonable for a person to use capital as income in their retirement, because they are going to die at some future time, it is not desirable for a state or country to do so—at least, not unless it sees death in the near future.

Eventually, of course, there will be no more capital to draw on and the real situation will become apparent. The dynamics of the system are such that, as capital exhaustion approaches, and as the rate of inflation increases exponentially as people try to maintain their spending power by more and more wage demands, eventually the system must collapse.

Capital is necessary in any monetary system, whether it be capitalist, communist or some other. Apart from an amount used as a buffer to even out supply and demand, capital is needed in industry. Without continual industrial investment there is no replacement and improvement of machines and factories, with a consequent reduction in production as efficiency decreases. This, of course, puts prices up and helps fuel inflation.

In a sense, some of the systems operating in the monetary world are similar to confidence tricks well known to police forces all over the world. The first one is 'the accumulator'. Here one sets up some form of business—tree-planting in a remote corner of the world used to be popular, pig-farming has also been tried. One advertises and gets people to invest at a high rate of interest, paying them out of new capital that has been attracted in. All the time that the system is growing it is possible to continue. Eventually, of course, one runs out of people and the system collapses. If one has judged it right one disappears with the funds just before the downward part of the graph sets in. If one plans such a system carefully one can match it with the growth rate for the population, in which case one can keep going until such time as population peaks off. The systems dynamics are the same in both cases for, although one is giving interest, there is no real gain in wealth, therefore one will eventually give out all the capital taken in as interest if one does not quit at some point before this happens.

A very similar con trick is the chain letter, sometimes disguised as pyramid selling. Here *one* person starts a letter or sales organisation, getting *two* other people to spread the good news to *four* others, and so on, all the while feeding money back to the original source. Exponential growth occurs until there is saturation, at which point the scheme crashes.

How, then, can one achieve real growth in the wealth of a community? There are two ways in which this has occurred in the past. Firstly, one can open up new lands, or dig deeper for mineral deposits in the old. Eventually this must cease, and by and large it is beginning to slow down now. With the exception of the USSR, Brazil and Canada there is little new land worth opening up, not without expensive irrigation at least. The same is true with mineral deposits: eventually these will be used up and growth must cease.

There is, however, one way left, which may be open ended so far as we can see at present, and that is the development of technology. Technology *per se* will not increase wealth; it can, in fact, have precisely the opposite effect, for it is no magic formula by itself. However, the planned application of technology to problems has historically had its effect. Every invention that has saved time, or enabled Man to do things that were not possible before, has added to the wealth of the community, for wealth is partly a question of goods and services divided by time. Thus, if a weaver can make things ten times faster with a new loom, then he will get ten times as rich—or, more likely, overproduce, so reducing the price of his goods so that everybody becomes that much richer. This, in its early days at least, formed the history of technology: it produced cheaper, more useful or more durable goods, the benefits of which were shared out in a rough and ready way throughout the community. The patent legislation recognised this, and gave the inventor a limited time in which to make such gains as he could before the invention was merged with the general body of knowledge which all could draw on. The development of factories during the Industrial Revolution greatly accelerated this process, with machines for making and packaging items multiplying, in some cases, a person's productivity by a thousandfold.

The process, however, is a dynamic one. Inventions have a certain lifetime and once they have exceeded that they tend to have a negative effect. If one slows down the rate of invention one has a similar effect to that seen when a wave runs into shallowing water: it humps up and threatens to break. In the same way, many inventions—or results of inventions made in the boom days of the Industrial Revolution—are now threatening to break on our society. This is not to say that we must be forever engaged in some accelerating race against the ill-effects of our past inventions; it should be possible to get a steady state if desired, or to vary the rate within limits, once one has understood the processes operating.

Technology is not immune to the faults of the monetary system as a whole. It is possible to have it going in the wrong direction, chasing profits which just do not exist, and which can be seen not to exist if one examines the system closely. In the past there has been a certain euphoria about technology, as though it were some formula which could be applied and always give beneficial results. This, unfortunately, is not so.

It is possible to spend money unwisely so as to reduce the total wealth of the community as well as to spend it to give a gain. To quote a simple example, it is possible to spend for a house £600 ($1200) on a central heating system which will thereafter cost £150 ($300) a year to run; or one could spend £300 ($600) on insulation and end up with a running cost of only £100 ($200) a year. Similar examples can be found on an international scale. The British and French Government's decision to go ahead with the Concorde project may well be such an example. At best, only a few people will fly in it, for a saving of only a few percent of their travelling time, and even then they would not use the craft if they had to pay the full cost of the fare. To get any money back out of the scheme the initial costs must be written off and, maybe, the seats subsidised into the bargain. In this case the prime consideration was not one of economy—the airbus scheme was around at the same time, and was obviously a better bet regarding cheap transport. However, prestige can be costed, too, and in this case it was probably not worth the investment. For less than one-thousandth of the total investment it would have been possible to develop a cheap electric bicycle that would have provided short-haul transport for millions, and a huge export potential that would have lasted well into the time of acute fuel shortage that is ahead. Or, if one wants to write off huge amounts of capital to provide jobs, the Severn Barrage could have been built and amortised, thus providing cheap electricity virtually forever.

It is not enough to say that high technology develops new techniques and products, thus giving a spinoff that benefits the community at large; true, it often does so, but similar spinoffs can also occur from intermediate technology and, in any case, the problems are identifiable and could be solved at less cost by a direct approach. This is not to say that high technology is wrong, merely that it should be costed more effectively before a major scheme is undertaken. Otherwise it may lead to a reduction in the wealth of the community and reduce its capacity to undertake any technology, high or low.

A similar situation exists with the development of atomic energy. At the present time the cost of electricity from an atomic reactor is not known, simply because the cost of storing the waste (or the cost of failing to store it adequately) is not known. It is very doubtful if atomic energy is at all competitive with other forms of power in terms of technology geared to the reduction in the use of power by using it more efficiently. It is possible that the true cost will be greater than the benefit that will accrue from its use, so we again would have negative technological advance, which costs more than it is worth.

This is not true, however, of fusion research: there is hope that abundant clean power could be produced from this. At the present time it still looks a worthwhile investment. Maybe it will be found impossible and we will lose all or most of the investment money, but that is one of the risks of pushing into new ground: so long as the average gain from technological advance exceeds the overall cost, it is worth the effort. For every oilwell that produces oil there are twenty dry holes. Technology is doing quite a bit better than this at the present time.

Observably, over the past few centuries, the income from new inventions and discoveries has exceeded the amount of time and money spent on them. If this were not so then there would have been no rise in the standard of living. Whether the amount of capital taken out of the system by inventors has exceeded the amount they have put in is doubtful. The average inventor spends much of his lifetime engaged in new ideas—quite often it is an overriding obsession, perhaps because those not of this temperament quit early on and drop from sight. Although, in many cases, the inventor's invention may save or generate hundreds of millions of pounds in his lifetime, he gets nothing or less than nothing from it.

From the point of view of the system as a whole there is a very good case indeed for incentives to invention. This may lead to some very rich men, but this does not matter so long as they create wealth that is dispersed through the community. In the rare cases where inventors have amassed vast fortunes much was ploughed straight back in again by way of further invention, probably in the most efficient manner as the inventors were in the best position to judge where to spend it most effectively.

If we fail to develop methods to ascertain whether an invention will give real benefit to the community, and fail to develop methods of incentives for inventors, then the rate of technological advance will slow as more and more unprofitable schemes are followed. This will fuel inflation and lead to the ultimate collapse of the system, which is already strained by disequilibrium in other areas.

In any scheme of social organisation the primary goal must be to create wealth; how it is shared out among the community is a secondary consideration. Any scheme which is primarily concerned with distribution must ultimately fail when it runs out of wealth to distribute. The danger is that activities which effectively act as distributive agencies may masquerade as activities which create wealth. Thus one often hears the argument that a new industry will 'create jobs'. The function of an industry is not, however, to create jobs, surprising as this may seem: its function is to provide goods and services, and the less work that goes into the creation of those goods and services the better in terms of the overall efficiency of the system. Once an industry tips the other way and starts creating work to a greater degree than it saves work in other areas, then it becomes a drain on the community. The idea that people must be found work—whether it is productive or not—stems probably from the Puritan ethic that work is inherently good, compounded with a political fear of being unemployed. There is no real justification in making work for the sake of it, for there is plenty of real work to be done and plenty of cost-effective operations that can be undertaken without recourse to spurious industry. True, there is the organisational problem of channelling work in the right direction, but this is essentially a subsystem of the whole and must be subservient to it. Trying to solve the problem in a way which reduces the efficiency of the system will lead only to worse situations later. If it really is impossible to create viable industry, then it would be better to reduce working hours across the board and maybe bring down the age of retirement, rather than keep people busy doing essentially nothing.

Exactly what proportion of the work done in an industrial country is *nonwork*, in the sense that there is no gain, or *anti-work*, in the sense that it creates more work for others, again with no gain, is not known exactly. Probably it is a large fraction, as the apparent gains in speed and efficiency in industry are less impressive if compared to the gains of the community as a whole.

Basically, there are two ways of getting rich. One can either create or discover new wealth or one can accumulate other peoples'. This acquiring of other peoples' wealth is perhaps the major objection to the capitalist system; tax systems are designed to give a more equable distribution. Unfortunately, no tax system makes any discrimination between created and accumulated wealth, and this tends to remove wealth from hands which might otherwise use it to create more. Thus it might at some point be worth trying to devise a system which gave incentives to new wealth. One could do this by having a tax-free period for new industry, or full repayment of development cost once a new invention was demonstrably increasing the wealth of the community. It should be noted at this point that what is true for the individual is not necessarily true for the nation, for, whereas one individual may get rich at the expense of his fellows, not everyone can. Thus a nation can increase its wealth only by creating new wealth—unless it is in a position to collect that of other nations and, even then, on the world scale there can be no real gain by altering the distribution.

This brings us to the question of what should be done with discovered wealth. In some ways this is different from created wealth, although the two are linked. Discovered wealth in the form of mineral deposits or fuel is not renewable, whereas there is no prospective end to the wealth that may be created by the application of intelligence to technological extension.

Discovered wealth is a form of capital, and should be treated as such. It is unwise to use it as income and ideally it should be translated into other forms of capital so that it will continue to exist and be of benefit. Here there is some difficulty in deciding what is capital. Normal rules no longer apply over the time base one has to work on. Obviously extracting petrol and burning it in a car is using it as a form of income, shortly to be expended. Employing it to build a dam or a canal might be a better use, particularly if the dam can generate more power than was used in its construction. Ultimately, however, dams fracture or their lakes silt up, and canals reduce in usefulness as trade routes alter or ship construction overtakes their capacity.

Probably the only true conversion we can make is to convert such wealth to knowledge because, for so long as a community exists in a form capable of understanding and using its knowledge, it will benefit by it. Thus, if the use of fuel relieves people from toil in the fields, some of them should be employed in advancing the knowledge of the community in institutions of learning or research; thus the mineral capital will be used but will in part be effective in advancing the technology so that it is able to survive once the fuel has gone. If it is all spent on raising standards of living and reducing working hours (or effective working hours—the two are not the same thing), then our last state will be worse than our first, for we will have a greater population, with a greater expectation, to be supported on a depleted resource base.

Obviously this process has to some extent occurred, but whether it has occurred in the right degree is doubtful. By and large we have used our capital to increase the size of our civilisation and to increase the wealth of its individuals more than we have used it to increase the corporate wealth by way of knowledge, or to enhance its value by way of new ethics and ideas.

11 Food

Much has been said in recent years about the world's inability to grow food for its increasing population. Now that grain stocks are nearing exhaustion the position is becoming more critical and there are several things that may happen.

The most obvious is, of course, widespread famine and a rapid decline of the population to the carrying level; however, the extent of this famine is by no means easy to predict, for there are several options that may alleviate the worst of its effects.

Firstly, beef and dairy production will start to give way to arable production, as the tonnage per acre gained this way is far greater than by using animals as intermediates. The conversion factor for animals is very roughly 10%; thus 90% of the food eaten by an animal is lost. After this, improved strains of plants could be used to increase food production from a given acreage. Progress in this direction is slow but steady and there is hope that most plants can continue to be improved in this way. The soya bean, for example, is virtually a wild plant and yields are low compared to other similar species. There are, of course, considerable dangers in going for culture of a single strain: the statistics are such that sooner or later we are likely to suffer from the effects of its becoming suddenly virtually extinct. Extreme pressure on food supply might lead to the situation where nobody grows a variety that is slightly less profitable, as by so doing they will be subsidising everybody else's security by having a reduced crop. With good planning and legislation, however, this situation could easily be avoided.

A more insidious danger is the replacement of wild strains by a single or small number of cultivated ones. A wild plant can be considered as a bunch of keys, each one able to unlock a particular environmental problem, whether it be drought, frost resistance, immunity from fungal attack or maybe a higher percentage of protein in the seed. A cultivated plant, while being very good at solving the problem it is bred for, does not have this variety of attributes. Thus, by destroying wild species, one is throwing away solutions to problems that have not yet arisen. Once these species have gone there is little hope of retrieving them, for the plant took several hundreds of millions of years to evolve and one cannot compress that kind of timescale into a five-year plan. The very fact that a wild plant has lasted so long speaks for its adaptability. During the lifetime of its species it is likely to have experienced the worst that fate can throw against it and come out on top. Contrast this with the life expectancy of the average garden strain and one can see the scale of the problem.

One of the most likely developments resulting from a threatened or actual shortage of food is an increase in production by any means available. At present food production is limited to the use of only parts of plants: if more of the plant could be used as food, then production could be increased proportionately. There are several routes to this, the simplest being the chemical cracking of cellulose, which makes up the bulk of plant tissue, to derive sugar. Another route would be to use the inedible portions as feedstock for algae or other single-celled organisms.

The use of algae direct might be a more satisfactory solution. Plants are inefficient as collectors of solar energy, and they have a slow growth rate. Algae can absorb many times the amount of energy out of a given amount of sunlight than higher plants can, and some have a doubling rate of the order of hours rather than weeks. Further, many of them yield higher concentrations of protein than the higher plants. Because they live in a liquid environment, handling problems are simpler—the liquid can be pumped, filtered and evaporated in a way that is not possible in normal farming. Indeed, the tank farm of the future will probably resemble an oil refinery more closely than anything else.

There are other plants, yeasts and fungi, that do not get their energy from sunlight.

Some yeasts can live on crude oil (the breakdown of oil in the sea is effected by micro-organisms, mostly, as yet, not too well identified). The technique of growing yeasts in oil was first developed as a way of cleaning water from the heat exchangers of oil refineries, and later to clean the oil itself of impurities such as nitrogenous and sulphur compounds. It is not a far step from this to the adding of substances to the oil to improve the yeast crop and make this the main product. At the present time there is great interest in this possible route to food production, with particular reference to those organisms that can live on the paraffin series and convert some of the energy stored in oil to fats and proteins. This is probably one of the main areas of expansion for food technology —and, in some ways, it could be the least desirable.

The advantages of the technique are that the oil companies have the capital and expertise to develop the process quickly. They have good cash incentives, for a modern chemical plant lends itself to the production of a large volume of high-purity product. Thus, in the next twenty years, we could see the development of refineries, similar in some ways to present-day oil refineries, producing food that would otherwise take thousands of square kilometres of land to produce. The costs are likely to go down as well. Refineries are sophisticated places where one man can produce an end-product measured in thousands of tonnes over the period of a year; they can be made virtually automatic, with very tight quality control.

With the present shortage of food, rising prices and lack of other investment opportunities it is almost inevitable that 'food factories' of this nature will spread rapidly. At first the produce will probably be fed to animals, but before long it will be doctored and textured so as to be acceptable straight from factory to table. Again there is a cash incentive, for by using animals much of the food will be lost, to say nothing of the expense of running a farm. As food prices rise people will be more ready to accept a substitute for some of the dishes they are accustomed to at the moment, particularly when the alternative is starvation.

What, then, of the dangers? The obvious one is, of course, that by using oil as a feedstock to the food industry we are still hooked on fossil-fuel reserves, and any additional use by way of food can only bring their exhaustion nearer in time. Thus, by the time the oil runs out, we could have half the world dependent on it for food. True, there are tar sands and shale oils that, while not commercially viable for fuel, might well be so for food. All this, however, is a matter of degree: by making ourselves dependent on limited fossil resources for food we would be putting ourselves in the position of a maggot eating its way through an apple, with the proviso that we, unlike the maggot, cannot grow wings and fly away.

The dangers are not so much in the developing of the new technology but in its being developed in an uneven manner, so that it is totally oil-orientated, leaving a perhaps unbridgeable gap when the oil runs out. What could be done is to use some of the profits from the easy high-yield oil process to develop the less attractive hydroponic process and ultimately, perhaps, techniques for the direct synthesis of food from inorganic material. If this were done then it would be a relatively simple process to phase oil out gradually and replace it with an 'in cycle' method.

Even were this achieved, there is still one major danger to be faced. The concentration of food production in factories will be of the same order of significance as the replacement of hunting by agriculture. The carrying capacity of the land will go up a hundredfold, and at the same time vast tracts of land will no longer be needed for agriculture. Thus the cities will be free to expand virtually until they meet each others' boundaries. In short, the development of synthetic food is likely to lead to a population explosion that will make the present one look like a damp squib.

This, of course, will throw severe strains on the other resources of the planet. Metal and energy shortages will become more acute, pollution will become much more widespread and interest in it will decline for a while as it no longer threatens the food base. We could even end up in the ridiculous situation where cities are domed and have their own air-conditioning plants, all waste being dumped outside with no further thought for the environment. We would then, to all intents and purposes, be living on an alien planet, because that is what we would have made it.

This, of course, is speculation. However, at the present time refineries are being adapted to make food from oil and production is already in the thousand tonne per annum range. It is certain that this food will form an increasing part of the diet of humans. There is a very high probability that progress in this field will outstrip the alternatives, and before very long may begin to show up in the guise of a drop in value of marginal agricultural land. Thus, the pattern is to some extent set. What we need now is some kind of system that will ensure that development proceeds across the board, and that it is not concentrated in the one area where failure can be confidently expected within less than a lifetime.

12 Climate

The climate is always changing. During the history of the world pretty well all types of climate seem to have occurred in most places. This is of fundamental importance to living creatures, for they are all dependent on solar energy trapped by green plants. When conditions are favourable for plants then everything dependent on them does well too; when they are not so favourable everything else suffers.

This is true for us also. The first civilisations arose in areas where a lot of food could be gathered for a little effort, leaving time to spare for other things, such as buildings, roads, armies and empires. Thus it is possible to look at our historical achievements in the light of the climatic conditions that made them possible. Perhaps it was not our unaided efforts that brought forward successive waves of civilisation but an improving climate that meant the carrying capacity of the land increased, as also the area suitable for human habitation. This is a less flattering view of human progress, but probably nearer the truth; certainly we are subject to fluctuations in the climate just as much as are other species, and if it turns against us we must either move out to better regions or end up a bit thinner on the ground.

At present the climate is showing a definite regression. We are, perhaps, about two-thirds of the way towards the next glacial period, and there is likely to be a steady deterioration in climate over the next thousand years. We seem currently to be enjoying an interglacial period in an Ice Age that has already lasted for some two million years.

The causes of these natural cycles in the climate are not fully understood. One probable cause is a fluctuation in the output from the Sun. Many stars show obvious periods of increased brightness: some run to a cycle of a few minutes, hours or days, others take many years. It is quite possible that most, if not all, stars have long-term minor fluctuations that are not so easy to detect. The inside of a star is a turmoil of convection currents boiling up through hot plasma and, although in some ways the mechanics of this are simple, there must to some extent be random or cyclic fluctuations.

Alternatively, the cause of climatic fluctuation could be here on Earth. The atmosphere is an absorber of much of the Sun's energy, either directly or by contact with the heated surface of the Earth; any changes in the constitution of the atmosphere are bound to have their effect on its capacity to absorb or reject heat, which in turn affects our climate.

There are two main factors which have come in for attention in the past few years. Firstly, there is a much greater quantity of carbon dioxide around than there was at the beginning of the century, and we are likely to double this before the beginning of the next. Up to a point the atmosphere is 'buffered' by the fact that carbon dioxide is highly soluble in sea water, so that most of the excess will end up in the sea. The sea itself is buffered also by the vast amount of limestone (calcium carbonate) present in coral reefs. Thus if extra carbon dioxide appears in the air, it will eventually end up in calcium bicarbonate formed from the combination of the limestone, as the reefs dissolve, with the carbon-dioxide-bearing water. The process takes time, however, and we are producing carbon dioxide at a far greater rate than it is being removed; thus the atmospheric concentration is increasing.

The known effect of carbon dioxide is that it reduces loss from the atmosphere of infrared (or heat) radiation: it produces a 'greenhouse effect' which could be expected to warm up the world slightly as the carbon-dioxide concentration increased. However, all the evidence suggests that the world is cooling down, so some other factor must be looked for. A likely one is dust. Small particles swept up into the upper atmosphere tend to form a reflective layer, the more so as some of them act as nuclei for water-droplet formation, so that heat from the Sun is reflected directly back into space. Certainly there is a lot more dust than there used to be— virtually half the industrial processes operating produce atmospheric pollution in one form or another, and on top of this there is a considerable input from farming.

The results of this cooling are already with us. They are evidenced in a reduction of rainfall in a belt either side of the equator and a reduction in the growing season further north. This must lead to a reduction in food output and an increase in the fuel used for heating. There are, of course, minor fluctuations imposed on the general trend, but our present state of knowledge indicates that the trend has set in and will be with us for some time yet.

One further factor which might possibly affect rainfall is the distribution of oil on the surface waters of the oceans. This reduces evaporation, which might mean that the air is drier, and thus less likely to deliver the same rainfall, than it would otherwise be. The area covered is not known accurately. Certainly several millions of tonnes are spilt annually, not only from ship spills—these have reduced lately: a good half of it is sump oil from land vehicles. Against this, the amount needed to give a complete layer a single molecule thick under ideal conditions is only about twenty thousand tonnes. Probably this cause already has some effect, and obviously there will come a point when it becomes a major factor in climate.

If the causes of climatic change are here on Earth there is much we can do to correct them. Dust could be reduced considerably by pollution control in industry while different farming practices could reduce the agricultural input—which is in any case undesirable as loss of topsoil reduces fertility. Not much can be done about atmospheric carbon dioxide, although fortunately its increase may act in our favour in any case. Some compensatory effect could come in increased plant growth, but this will probably be more than offset as the last great forests are destroyed, with the consequent oxidation of the carbon in them and the oxidation of the underlying minerals. Oil pollution could be minimised by tighter controls and recycling. A big boost in this direction could come from legislation to ensure that recycled oil is untaxed, the premise being that tax has been paid once and any subsequent re-use should not be re-eligible for tax. This would greatly increase the cash value of the oil and make its recycling a much more attractive proposition. The redesign of engine sumps, so that they were effectively the container in which the oil was bought, would also help. To change the oil one would merely remove the container and replace it with another one, thus speeding service time and reducing the risk of spillage.

Freons, used as aerosol propellants, have been mentioned many times as a factor in climatic change. Probably their use will be banned in the near future.

It is interesting to note that the Earth's atmospheric envelope is considerably different from those surrounding its neighbours.

Of the two nearest, Mars appears to be running slower than us, probably as a result of its smaller size. So far as we can make out it is only just getting to the stage of outgassing from the core as the planet heats up from radioactive decay and releases gas. As its gravity is less than ours it could not hold such a big envelope in any case. Alternatively, Mars may once have had a reasonably rich atmosphere but may have been unable to retain it owing to the weakness of the planet's gravity.

Venus, on the other hand, although slightly smaller than the Earth, has a very dense atmosphere with high temperatures and pressures at the bottom. It may be that the Earth's atmosphere could be 'tipped over the top', so to speak. If it got too hot the oceans would evaporate and produce such a cloud cover that the top of this, rather than the land surface, would be the effective radiative surface. We would then have an atmosphere very similar to that of Venus—at least so far as depth and pressure were concerned. It may be that both states are stable, for once this had occurred it is difficult to postulate a mechanism that would cool it down again to the present stable state. Although no problem at present, it might be something to be borne in mind if we start to produce increasing thermal pollution from atomic power stations.

13 Education for the Future

Most teachers, if pressed, will make some claim to the effect that they are 'educating children for the future'. Although a laudable objective, there is little evidence that this is the case. In the absence of any clear idea of what the future will be like, most schools in fact educate children for the past.

Hitherto this has not mattered so much, for the future was in many respects like the past. There was some hope of improvement in certain areas, but the main elements were recognisable both sides of the present. Now this is becoming less so. The future is going to be very different from the past and many of our accepted values and landmarks will go.

At present there is a very real need for futures education in schools. It is doubtful if the kind of education we are at present giving will be in any way adequate to deal with the problems that children will have to face before they are halfway through their lives. If we get it wrong, there is a good chance that most of the children now in schools will also get it wrong when they are trying to make effective decisions in twenty years or so. At all events, the period of adjustment is likely to be harder if they have no idea of what the future is likely to yield, and what it could be like. All schools teach history; there is an equally good case for teaching the future.

In some ways schools, hospitals and prisons are similar. They are institutions designed to normalise people, or, failing that, to detain them so that those who do not conform are not mixed with the rest of society. At first only prisons performed this function, then mental hospitals were set up, and now schools are beginning to perform a similar function as the school leaving age is raised and parents spend more time at work. By extrapolation we could eventually see them all merged into some 'ministry of people', a perhaps undesirable rationalisation.

One problem is that the two functions of detention and normalisation are dissimilar, and it is difficult to carry out the two processes at the same time with mixed groups. Quite often the detained group has an adverse effect on the other and the efficiency of the process declines. In juvenile detention centres the introduction of the first offender to more experienced criminals leads to a rapid cultural exchange, which results in the first offender acquiring the language, methods and mentality of crime. Similarly, mental hospitals can institutionalise their inmates to such an extent that they are no longer able to function outside, even if they are cured of the original illness. Schools are now feeling similar pressures. In any school there is a sector of the population that is there only because it is required to be so by law. These young people are in fact detainees because there are no jobs outside —or, if they did find jobs, they would decrease those available for the adult population. Naturally this breeds resentment which leads to behavioural difficulties that throw an increasing burden on the rest of the structure, reducing its efficiency. Worse still, it is beginning to breed resentment also on the part of those who *want* to learn.Thus a system of compulsory, equal education for all, designed to reduce social tensions, may well have exactly the opposite effect as the educable and able are thrust in closer proximity to the less educable and less able.

In a society where wages for the unskilled have risen much faster than those for the skilled, coupled with the increasing workload thrust on the skilled as their services are more in demand, we have a danger that the skilled will eventually reach a point where they decide they are not going to play this particular game any more. Probably this will come about when it is realised that a system breakdown is imminent. So long as there is hope for a better future, people will slog on under very adverse conditions; if they know things are not going to improve they will quit sooner. This opting out is already evident in US education, where the brightest people tend not to take degrees any more. In the UK the pace is

71

slower, but there are few doctors or teachers who advise their children to follow in their footsteps.

This divisive factor in society is undesirable and tends to perpetuate class philosophy. Not that there is anything wrong with gradations in society *per se*: there are bound to be some kind of levels in any society, largely as a result of differences in ambition and ability. However, they can have the effect of absorbing too much attention and interest so that more important considerations get lost. In the UK in particular there has been considerable preoccupation with social class over the past half century. Unfortunately many of the measures meant to reduce differentials have, due to lack of futures planning, tended to exacerbate them.

One such attempt at class levelling which has been in operation for several decades is the council housing programme. Although in some areas more than 20% of the total housing is council-owned, the housing problem has not been solved in this way, but has instead become worse,

The dynamics of the system are quite simple. Obviously it is a good thing for people to be housed, and therefore it is good politics to house them. Thus one can argue that the building of council houses for those who cannot house themselves is a good thing. However, under the present system, although there are certain requirements to be met by people on the housing list, once they have gained possession there is no method of revision, after a given period of years, to see if a person still needs such housing. Thus an increasing number of people become entrenched in houses which they may no longer have any real claim on, while the needy are to be found in the back streets, waiting years for a council occupant to die or more houses to be built. Worse is yet to come, however, for that section of the population in council housing is effectively relieved of any need to make any input into the building industry, other than a small rent which seldom covers the cost of running the house. Instead they tend to spend on consumer items, thus encouraging these industries at the expense of housing. Further, the council subsidy comes from the other householders of the town, thus reducing *their* ability to make provision for themselves and forcing some out of the bottom of the private sector and into council housing. The system has a positive feedback and, by extrapolation, should lead to everybody occupying a council house—or, more realistically, occupying a place on the council waiting list, for the funds for new construction would dry up long before the last person was housed.

In addition to this, there are certain undesirable features concerning mobility for council tenants. Once in, one is trapped and thus council estates can become captive pools of labour, with, at least in some cases, a depression in the wages structure. Even without this, the brighter and more ambitious will be seriously impeded in chasing better jobs, for the difference between subsidised and unsubsidised housing can be £15 a week, which, with tax, means that it is not worth moving for any promotion of less than £1000 a year. Thus a person can be trapped and never start up a promotion ladder that he might otherwise scale. If we go further and examine the structure of inheritance, we find that council parents leave very little to their children, thus perpetuating the lack of capital and reducing the opportunity for the children to buy their own houses. Also the average number of children per family is greater on council estates, for the simple reason that having children is one of the qualifications for entry. It is unlikely that this situation has no effect on the breeding rate of the population waiting to get a council house, so we have one more undesirable feedback to the system.

One could make a very good case that the average working man is the victim of a system designed to provide an excess of labour. Thus he is encouraged to have a larger family than he might otherwise want in order to get a house. Once in, he is effectively prevented from moving in search of a better job. His children are deprived of any inheritance so that they too remain poor and are trapped in the system. Contraceptive knowledge is less readily available at the bottom end of the social spectrum. All these inputs certainly are not helpful to

73

him and, although there is little evidence that it is all part of a plot, it is perhaps not entirely accidental that they all converge in one area. At least this makes a change of viewpoint from the more common one that the poor make all their own troubles.

Thus, in considering an educational system for the future, it might be advisable to go back a little further than the classroom and examine the conditions and circumstances outside the school to a greater degree. This, of course, is true of any systems analysis: if the problems are not readily soluble in the immediate area under examination then one must go back further into the system to look for the disequilibrium elsewhere. Certainly where schools are having the least success in attaining their designed function it is found that the problems originate outside them, and these external problems can usually be traced to some few undesirable system inputs. This is not to say that the problems are simple, but it does at least give hope that they are soluble, which is perhaps a good enough expectation on which to take action.

14 Arms and Men

Virtually all countries have a defence force of some sort or another. Their function is, of course, to defend the country against the defence forces of other countries; there is a good reinforcement of the system and any country that tries to drop out is likely to get taken over by its neighbours. Therefore any attempt to get rid of defence forces is likely to fail in just the same way that any attempt to get industry to reduce pollution unilaterally will fail. In both cases, the dynamics of the system are against it.

There is, however, an obvious inducement to reduce expenditure on defence, for the defence industry is a spurious industry in that it has no useful end product and uses valuable materials and manpower. The drain on the economy is huge, and there is some evidence that eventually the cost of dominance will sap the energy of the dominator to the extent that some other country steps into first place. Thus the country that can get by with the least expenditure on defence is generally the most successful in improving trade and investment. Japan and Germany since the last war are good examples of this.

Sometimes the threat of war is given as a reason for having, or not having, a defence expenditure for a country. While it is true that defence expenditure does increase the risk of war, the risk is not necessarily linear, and there is the possibility of a stable situation. Unfortunately such stable periods are usually not more than a few decades in duration. Historically, wars are a minor threat to life—it may be that our preoccupation with them has made them bulk too large in the history books. If we look at the numbers killed in the last war, we find that any major tobacco company can claim more. If we look at the injuries, they are much less in extent than road casualties. If we look at the injustices, it all depends on the point of view: there is plenty of injustice in the world, both national and international, and quantitatively war is only a small offender.

Thus wars are really rather minor affairs if considered in the context of civilisation as a whole, but they capture the imagination and evoke an emotive response from people in a way that little else does. It is a game that most people can play and nearly all can be forced to play. Occasionally people break the rules, and maybe shoot their own officers instead of those on the other side, but by and large people accept them.

Whether this situation is likely to pertain in the future is doubtful. In just the way that our industrial efforts are larger in scope and have bigger effects on the environment than previously, future wars could be much more destructive and have longer lasting effects than before. This is perhaps not surprising as modern war is an offshoot of the industrial scene. Even without war there is a good chance that continuing high rates of expenditure on arms will so warp the structure and thinking of the civilisation that a war may in the end be superfluous, being more in the nature of a death rattle than a cause.

What then can be done to reduce the risks of the situation? One possible route would be to extend the function of the armed forces, rather than seek to diminish them. We have, after all, in the forces a highly organised, skilled and disciplined structure, quite often with some commitment to the preservation of a way of life, its standards, values and wealth. Also the people in charge are not fools and are used to thinking in terms of strategy in constantly changing circumstances.

One way of bringing this major investment back into profitability might be to make the game more real. First we should identify our enemies, and then consider what action we can most profitably take. This will require a considerably more detailed analysis than has been undertaken hitherto, for our enemies are not other people, or nations, but aspects of people and nations in general, their reactions to the environment and each other. Thus one major function of a defence

76

force should be to analyse the nature and causes of war and seek to reduce its probability. This could lead to some internationalisation of defence forces. In other fields, such as medicine, scientific research and industry, there is considerable exchange of information and cooperation in the face of problems. If the function of defence could be broadened, there might be a possibility of international conferences on defence —not defence against each other, but defence against common problems such as food shortage, fuel shortage, pollution, health hazards, resource shortages and so on. If progress were made in this field, there would be a greater chance of a reduction in armaments, for one would not be offering the choice of arms or no arms, with a consequent loss of jobs, but a choice of arms or some other more useful activity which would tend to strengthen the nation and thus render it more competitive. Moreover, there would be opportunity to examine real dangers further back in the dynamics of the situation. For example, a real threat to Europe might well be a massive Russian crop failure as a result of changing weather patterns. If this and the options devolving from it were discussed in detail at international defence conferences, the results could be useful in terms of understanding and might lead to a reduction of risk.

Similarly, if the function of the armed forces is to protect against destruction of life and property, it might be useful to ask them what can be done about such major negative contributions to society as smoking. It is probable that, with the kind of capital and expertise, plus flexibility, that the services have, they could tackle international problems of this magnitude. Also, there are similar problems in the Third World that might yield to this kind of heavy investment in the problem.

At all events, most nations of the world have a high proportion of their national product tied up in defence, and this investment is not profitable. The real problem is that the mandate for defence forces is too limited, being restricted virtually to fighting other defence forces. If the whole concept

of defence could be broadened to include real and fundamental threats, rather than the present game where one reacts
only to other people's reactions to these threats and then tries
to destroy the people rather than the threat, then there is a
good chance of making this heavy investment profitable. If
this could be achieved the result would be dramatic, as there
is a large amount of material and manpower involved. Further,
there could be a considerable increase in morale of both the
services and the civilian population if the feeling that real
problems were being tackled and overcome was in the air.

15 Scale

Everyone is familiar with the idea of scale. Apart from the generalisation that bigger (or smaller) is better, most people realise that one can alter the size of a thing and in so doing alter other characteristics also. What is sometimes not realised is that a simple alteration in size may have a complex result which is not directly proportional to the change in size.

The problem is that, in changing scale, one alters only one characteristic, so that the balance of the others is altered in the process.

For example, one can consider the problem of scaling a human being. It is easy to postulate a person three metres tall, but if they are going to retain human proportion they must be twice as wide and twice as deep also. This leads to a person with, not double, but *eight times* the weight of an average person half the height. If we examine the bones in the leg that have to support this weight, we find that they have only four times the cross-section area, and so we end up with twice the loading. If we examine the heart, we find that it has eight times the blood volume to pump, over twice the distance. However, the blood vessels have only four times the cross-section so it must travel four times as fast. This of course means that the friction on the walls is greater, and we might find that we need four times the energy to double the speed. Thus the heart may end up having to do thirty-two times as much work. We run into similar problems when we examine the lung surface area in relation to the gas transfer required, the loadings that occur when our hypothetical giant falls over, and so on.

We end up with the conclusion that a person three metres tall probably could not be made to work. Certainly the maximum recorded height is only about two and a half metres, which is some evidence in our favour. Of course, one could go on to redesign completely, but one would probably end up with a leg at each corner and considerable relative variation of the sizes of bones and organs, rather than a simple scale model.

Although we can alter the size of living things hypothetically, and manufactured things in reality, we can do nothing about the gravitational field in which they operate, the rate of time flow, the strength of the materials of which they are composed and a host of other factors. If we could scale *everything* in a given environment, there would be in fact no way of telling if scaling had occurred, for all the ratios and relationships would be as before.

Most engineers are aware of the problems involved in scaling. Quite often there is a real gain in efficiency and in many ways it is true that bigger is better. However, in all things there must be an optimum, and in many cases one may suffer from some 'overshoot' once size is followed on the blind assumption that it is only the size, and not the relationship of size to other factors, that gives the increase in efficiency. More important still, we must learn to make a distinction between efficiency and function. This may seem an unnecessary distinction at first glance, but efficiency is usually related to a particular system or subsystem and not to the whole. It depends, of course, on one's point of view, and it is only with a holistic approach that one is likely to maintain overall efficiency while dealing with the separate parts.

For example, we can look for improvements in building practice and see how efficiency can be improved there. One might expect considerable gains as a result, because building is an old industry which has in some respects tended to fossilise at a lower level of technology than more recent industries. Firstly, we can consider the building as a cell, and in many ways the development of buildings is analogous to the development of cells. Initially all living cells were separate entities, but later the gains from incomplete mitosis conferred an advantage and an extension of the process led to the multi-million celled entities that largely populate the world as plants and animals today.

Thus we can say that two rooms are better than one and develop some specialisation of room function, as is found in the average house today. Initially every house had its own or shared nearby water supply and provided its own light by way of dips or candles. The big estates and their great houses probably represented the ultimate in this kind of organised self-dependence. Towns, however, became a more viable way of life than the great houses, as they had more specialised buildings by way of bakeries, leather workshops, and manu-factories of all kinds—also they provided a choice of employ-ment and wages.

With the coming of piped water, gas, electricity and the telephone, the separate houses became more and more linked by a common web of services. By extrapolation, we can expect communal heating, perhaps two-way television and an exten-sion of service industries within the near future. Already we are seeing the merging of individual houses by way of large apartment blocks and eventually we may arrive at a 'total building concept' where there is planning by the five-hectare lot, with all possible services contained under one roof or at least in an interlinked complex. In such a building one is approaching the 'unit village' and one can extrapolate to a 'unit town', which would be one large building.

Obviously one would begin to run into problems of heating, cooling, lighting and ventilation as one increased the size, but these problems could be solved in a variety of ways. One could bury the services in the interior of buildings, and com-puterise them so that they were more or less automatic. Industry could be put underground, for already much of it is conducted in artificial light. Entertainment could also be internalised, so that there would be little need or reason for a person to leave the building. Better communications would further reduce the need for mobility, which would lead to a greater packing density and efficiency, canteen meals would eliminate the need for separate kitchens, and sophisticated furniture design would free more floorspace, reducing the total required per person. An interesting feature of such a complex and interwoven system is that it would begin to exhibit many of the characteristics of a living organism, not the least being that it could die.

At this point one could say that the town had begun to take over, for efficiency has ousted function and the town is beginning to serve its own need rather than those of its occupants.

A similar process may be seen in the operation of the state. There are of course great gains in efficiency to be made by increasing the power and organisation of the state, but the efficiency is in favour of the state, not of its individual citizens. The efficient state does not increase the freedom or standard of living of its members, although it may be necessary to hold out a promise of this initially in order to get people to cooperate.

This does not mean that highly complex and highly organised towns or states are bad. It depends on where one places one's values. The problem is not that it is difficult or impossible to organise such a state—it could be done, and pressures on fuel and power might make it seem desirable— it is whether we want it, and, at a deeper level, whether it is a viable pathway from the evolutionary point of view. The most obvious trap is that it may lead to fossilisation at one particular level of organisation. In such a system feedback could be organised to give a very high degree of stability, so that it became impossible for individuals to have any significant effect on the direction the state took. It is axiomatic that living fossils are only waiting to become dead ones. The longer they survive without change, the greater their imbalance with changes occurring in the world at large, so that eventually they have to leave their safe niche and meet conditions with which they cannot contend. Thus the monolithic, stable state, although in some ways reassuring—and apart from questions of whether it is a good place to live in or not—contains inherent dangers which are not to be found in the more open, polymorphous type of organisation that can be considered its alternative.

16 An Alternative View

Although quantitative predictions for the future are relatively recent, qualitative ones are not. Religion, particularly the Christian religion, predicts a final state for the world, in which all ills are banished in the Millennium or 'thousand year rule'. After this there is a further unknowable qualitative leap into some other state once the world has ceased to exist

This is a central theme of the Christian religion, and to some extent it is perhaps a model for futurist thought. The intention is to improve the lot of Man, and to some extent the advance in knowledge has made progress in this direction.

This advance has had its feedback on religious thought. The trend is called secularisation, and basically it is the evolution of religion from myth, magic and mystery to more pragmatic, knowable realities. To some this is a process of debunking, the ultimate end of which will be the elimination of religion as the real world becomes more and more known, leaving less and less unknowns attributable to divine action. This is a simplistic view, however, derived from the mechanistic philosophies of the last century. Since then we have come to realise that the world is not as mechanistic as was once thought, and are beginning to realise that the philosophical methods that questioned religion can just as easily be applied to science. Thus we are now becoming aware that what were once thought to be unalterable scientific laws in fact represent only a fragment of reality, and that they tend to change in time. Some people doubt even that there is an unalterable reality, which we catch glimpses of; one can equally argue that what we are seeing is in part created by us. Leaving this aside, however, there is certainly some kind of evolutionary process occurring in both scientific and religious thought and if we extrapolate the trends we may be able to get some idea of where they are leading.

Trends usually have limits, and we can apply this rule

tentatively here. If both science and religion do in fact describe the real world, they must ultimately fuse in the manner in which they describe it—or, at least, knowledge must become more transactable one to the other. There is little point in trying rigidly to maintain some sort of Occam's razor here, for if one is to be really honest one must use the more modern equivalent of Occam's razor, the type with a cutting edge both sides, and say that in all probability results from both are mostly wrong when viewed from the standpoint of the future.

From this we can derive that, if the Church is right and we shall eventually enter the Millennium, we should be able to pick up some signs of it beforehand. One such indicator would be a growing together of science and religion into a more overlapping body of knowledge, and there is some slight evidence that this may be occurring. Another more immediate indicator might be the state of the Church. The function of the Church is to spread the message and perform some kind of holding operation until the return of Christ. After this event it will be about as useful as a spent rocket booster, for it will have achieved its aims.

So far we can see that the Church has worked through several different phases of its existence. After its initial spread and consolidation it went through a sort of 'spiritual determinism' phase, where it dictated the ideas and actions of its members, more or less by prescription (or at least proscription); through a materialistic phase, where it had considerable financial power; to the present phase, where its influence is much more diffuse. Observably the Church has 'leaked' in the past century—its influence has spread from the walls of its buildings and the tight 'in groups' of its followers—and is doing so today to such an extent that non-Christians, in the purely technical sense, may exhibit behaviour and thought patterns that are difficult to distinguish from the Christian model (if one disregards the required performance of ritual and attendance); this is sometimes disturbing to the faithful, who occasionally try to disown or bring back the scattered flock. Thus secularisation is a two-way process: not only does the world leak into the Church but the Church leaks into the world, and this, in fact, is its designed function.

Religion, then, will probably continue to change and become more closely involved in the world; it will continue to interact with other modes of thinking, including science and futurology, and have its effect on the values presented there. It is likely to be of value inasmuch as it is a route to 'open' systems. Faith can be a useful attribute to the scientist on occasion. Confronted with incontrovertible evidence that the world is running down to some irrevocable state of total chaos, coupled with equally incontrovertible evidence that Man is only a complex automaton, and that the last morning of creation shall read what the first one wrote into his atoms in the beginning, he can still say: 'But I have signed no contract to believe any of this'—and thus continue the search for truth.

Religion is slow to change, partly perhaps in contrast to the change about it, but also because it cannot 'up anchor' from its historical roots and cannot completely overturn its theories in the way that science can. If this sometimes leads to impatience perhaps one should temper this with the thought that ultimately the structure and organisation that is the Church must make the final sacrifice and make itself redundant.

17 Alternative Technology

To come back to more practical matters, let us consider the alternatives in technology—for, if the Church thinks it has problems, these are nothing compared to those facing technology! Present-day technology, if continued, bids fair to use up all of its material base within the next hundred years or so. Most people nowadays take the artefacts of high and intermediate technology for granted. However, there is now an increasing interest in low technology—to be more exact, perhaps one should say 'low impact technology', for much low technology is more destructive than its more sophisticated counterpart: individual coal fires, for example, are nearly as inefficient, and create vastly more pollution, than a central electricity generating station; primitive agriculture can be more destructive of land than more modern techniques, with all their faults.

However, it is possible to design technology that is low in profile and impact; quite often the solutions proposed are elegant and sophisticated, as well as fulfilling their design function. Many supporters of low technology see it as an alternative to high technology; more realistically, the two are likely to exist side by side for some time to come, although, hopefully, high technology will reduce its environmental impact as it develops.

The main characteristics of low technology are that the capital outlay is generally low, environmental disruption is minimised, it is commonly labour-intensive (not really such a bad thing if one recognises the alternative as unemployment), and a stock economy is implicit in its functioning. At present most of its practitioners are skilled and dedicated people; it is unlikely that the average cross-section of the public could handle the technology effectively without some period of adjustment. However, this is true of any technology in its earlier stages, and it will doubtless become simpler to use as it progresses. There is no reason to suppose that it could not be made as simple to handle as our present high technology. Whereas the average town dweller might be rather at sea if asked to operate, say, a hydroponic garden running on wastes, it is an easily learned and enjoyable skill with room for some specialisation of labour.

The two main fields in which low technology is making the most active progress at present are those of energy generation and food production. Already solar panels, designed to trap the Sun's heat for water and space heating, are competitive with other forms of heating and will become more so as fuel costs rise. Wind generators for electricity are being developed in several countries and, in locations remote from power lines, are substantially cheaper than the required hookup would be. Hand-in-hand with this, there are gains to be made in the application of the power generated—more efficient lighting, plus thermal insulation, can drastically reduce the power demand for the average house, thus making the capital part of the high-technology alternative a greater fraction of the total cost and therefore less attractive. In addition to all this there is the absence of the pollution and environmental disruption caused by the power station, a cost which is not passed on to the consumer by way of the bill. It may be argued that if the true cost of power were charged, many low-technology routes would win hands down.

Methane manufacture is another route to power production. Many sewage plants run themselves on the gas they produce, and the idea of utilising this on a larger scale is attractive— unfortunately, if one considers it on a *per capita* of population basis, the yield is very low. However, there is also a gain by way of high-quality fertiliser from such plants where industrial effluent is not permitted to enter the sewers, and a reduction in pollution in other areas where the sewage would otherwise be discharged.

When looked at from the point of view of farming, the route becomes more attractive. Certainly the average farm could more than run itself on the energy produced if an

87

effective method of reacting waste material could be devised. This might perhaps be a more fruitful area to explore, for at present the production of food takes more energy by way of fertiliser and fuel input than it produces by way of calories. This is perhaps one of the most damning condemnations of high technology, for to convert in the space of a few short decades the major energy-*producing* industry of a nation into the major *user* is a notable achievement, particularly as it was done without really trying.

Ideas about methane are not new. Dalton did experiments on the gas in the early part of the last century, and cow-dung gasworks are in operation in India. Natural gas, of course, is derived from the decomposition of organic material that has been trapped awhile in the Earth's crust—in the case of major gas fields, it is probably a result of heat and pressure rather than of bacterial decay. At present there is need of research into the bacteria responsible for the more direct fermentation route, for it is probable that improved strains could give significantly better rates and yields than are commonly obtainable. The costs of a methane plant using fermentation are low: all one needs are a reactor vessel and a collector, pressures and temperatures are not much above ambient, and a wide variety of materials can be used both for construction and as feedstock once the plant is running. The alternative route, that of autolysis or temperature cracking, is not so attractive as a considerable amount of the available energy is used in heating, and the waste products are not nearly so useful; it is quicker, however, and can produce a liquid fuel similar to paraffin, so doubtless this route will be pursued also.

The latest development for sewage treatment ignores the methane potential as being insignificant; instead, the plant is designed to compost all material, including garden refuse and kitchen wastes, with a free supply of oxygen so that no methane is produced. The result is about seventy pounds of dry odourless compost per year, per person. The Clivus, as it is called, is bulky, and really needs a basement for it to be fitted. It costs more than the conventional toilet but, if considered as an alternative to sewage pipes and treatment plant, is quite economic, particularly where long pipe runs are required. Also, of course, it really does solve a problem, rather than just dumping it on someone else's doorstep as so many sewage schemes do.

There are many other aspects of low technology. They offer unique scope for the private inventor as they are usually of the scale that benefits more from individual effort than from a highly funded research team. It is to be hoped that low-impact technology will start to supplement, and then partially replace, its counterpart in the next few decades.

Some Further Reading

This book is intended merely to whet the appetite. For this reason the arguments in it have, in many cases, been given a less than full exposition. It is hoped that the reader will wish to follow up the unanswered questions in more detail. The books in the following list give a good general coverage of the field, and most of them give reference to further works.

Perhaps one of the best ways to keep abreast of the field, and also to meet other people of similar interests, is to join some society interested in futures. The World Future Society in the UK is a good starting point and full details can be got from David Berry, 45 Bromley Common, Bromley, Kent, and from the World Future Society, PO Box 30369, Bethesda Station, Washington DC 200014. From here one can be put in touch with other branches in other countries. There are many other societies, all with their own particular interest; most of them are represented among members of the WFS, and it is a simple matter to find a chain of contacts once one has taken the plunge and joined *something*, for most people who belong to societies belong to more than one.

The following book list is by no means exhaustive, as it is intended only to give a sample of what is available.

Clarke, Arthur C. *Profiles of the Future* (Gollancz (UK) 1962; Harper and Row (US) 1973)
Most people know Clarke from his science-fiction writings; here the same high standard of writing is found, with emphasis on what is possible to technology and what is not.

Commoner, Barry. *The Closing Circle: The Environmental Crisis and its Cure* (Knopf (US) 1971; Cape (UK) 1972)
This is one of the key books with regard to the ecological argument. Well documented, very readable, it deals with the impact of Western industrialised society on its support base. Not a bedtime book—it is, in places, too frightening.

Forrester, Jay. *World Dynamics* (Wright-Allen (US) 1971; Wright Allen Press (UK) 1972)
This book deals with computer projections to show interactions

of population, resources, pollution and industry during the next decades.

Fuller, Buckminster and Marks, Robert. *The Dymaxion World of Buckminster Fuller* (Doubleday)
'Bucky' probably needs no introduction. This book deals with his work in a simple manner with many photos and sketches of his prophecies and projects.

Kahn, Hermann and Weiner, Anthony. *The Year Two Thousand* (Macmillan (US) 1972; Collier-Macmillan (UK) 1968)
This is one of the early works on futures, and in some ways it may seem a bit dated now. Kahn is an industrial optimist, largely because his Hudson Institute was concerned mainly with industrial forecasting. It did good work in alerting industry to the future, however, and the book is still interesting reading.

Meadows, Donella and Meadows, Desmond. *The Limits to Growth* (Universe (US) 1972; Earth Island (UK) 1972)
This is the report on the Club of Rome's project on the predicament of mankind. It can be considered the classic exposé of the economic theory of growth. Well backed by charts and diagrams.

Montefiore, Hugh. *The Question Mark* (Collins (UK) 1969; reprinted with additional information as *Can Man Survive?* (Collins (UK) 1970)
A collection of essays by one of the leading religious thinkers. Highly readable and challenging.

Rocks, Laurence and Runyon, Richard. *The Energy Crisis* (Crown (US) 1972)
A detailed analysis of the energy crisis, with some possible solutions.

Schumacher, E. F. *Small is Beautiful: A study of Economics as if People Mattered* (Blond and Briggs (UK) 1973; Harper and Row (US) 1974)
The case for decentralisation of industry, dealienation of labour, and the reintroduction of human scale and values.

Skinner, B. F. *Walden Two* (Macmillan (US) 1960; Collier-Macmillan (UK) 1976)
Written in 1948, this book is about a commune where conditioning was used to create a behavioural Utopia (Skinner is a leading exponent of behaviourist psychology). With hindsight it is

difficult to see what all the fuss was about when it first came out. It was, perhaps, taken more seriously than the author intended. Anyway, the book is still good reading.

Teilhard de Chardin. *The Phenomenon of Man* (Harper and Row (US) 1959; Collins (UK) 1961)
This is the lifework of Teilhard, not easy reading in places but well worth the effort. The scope of the book is so large that it is difficult to summarise it in a few words.

Theobald, Robert. *Futures Conditional* (Bobbs Merrill Co (US) 1965)
A good introduction to futures, this book is a collection of readings; all readers are likely to find something of interest.

Thring, M. W. *Man, Machines and Tomorrow* (Routledge and Kegan Paul (UK) 1973)
Thring is an inventor with a wide grasp of the history of invention, its possibilities and its limitations. Well worth getting even if you never have had an idea in your life.

Toffler, Alvin. *Future Shock* (Random (US) 1970; Bodley Head (UK) 1970)
The main theme of the book is the acceleration of the rate of change and its impact on values and institutions. The book is well documented with many examples; its only drawback is that it is rather long, but it may be dipped into rather than read from cover to cover.

Ward, Barbara and Dubois, René. *Only One Earth* (Penguin Books (UK) 1972)
An analysis of where we went wrong and what we should do to retrieve the situation.

Magazines
The Futurist. The journal of the World Future Society in the USA. Perhaps the best for general reading. From Box 30369, Bethesda Station, Washington DC 200014.
The Ecologist. The leading magazine for ecology and related aspects. From 73 Molesworth Street, Wadebridge, Cornwall, UK.
Towards Survival. A 'mini-mag' that reports socially useful inputs, with articles of topical interest. From 79 Sutton Avenue, Eastern Green, Coventry, UK.
Journal of the New Alchemists. PO Box 432, Woods Hole, Massachusetts 02543, USA.

Index

INDEX

DATE DUE

AUTHOR		
Thompson, Alan E.		

TITLE		
Understanding futurology...		

DATE DUE	BORROWER'S NAME	ROOM NUMBER

Ohio Dominican College Library
1216 Sunbury Road
Columbus, Ohio 43219

DEMCO